ANCHORED
to the Savior

*A Guide to Understand Christian
Salvation and Redemption*

REV. PATRICK EDWIN HARRIS

WESTBOW
PRESS®
A DIVISION OF THOMAS NELSON
& ZONDERVAN

This book is a work of non-fiction. Unless otherwise noted, the author and the publisher make no explicit guarantees as to the accuracy of the information contained in this book and in some cases, names of people and places have been altered to protect their privacy.

WestBow Press books may be ordered through booksellers or by contacting:

WestBow Press
A Division of Thomas Nelson & Zondervan
1663 Liberty Drive
Bloomington, IN 47403
www.westbowpress.com
844-714-3454

Unless otherwise noted, scripture taken from the King James Version of the Bible.

Scripture marked (NKJV) taken from the New King James Version®. Copyright © 1982 by Thomas Nelson. Used by permission. All rights reserved.

ISBN: 978-1-6642-6774-9 (sc)
ISBN: 978-1-6642-6775-6 (hc)
ISBN: 978-1-6642-6773-2 (e)

Library of Congress Control Number: 2022909883

Print information available on the last page.

WestBow Press rev. date: 8/4/2022

Contents

Contents

To my partner in life and in Christ,
my wife, Aloma

Introduction

*For [no] other foundation can man lay
than that is laid, which is Jesus Christ.*
1 Corinthians 3:11

anchor *(noun)* something that serves to
hold an object

When a house is being built, it is best to pour a concrete slab to act as an immovable foundation. So the builder will place curved metal bolts in wet concrete. These anchor bolts are hardened into the foundation and attach the house's wood frame to the concrete base with its rocklike nature. Thus the house is anchored to the foundation and becomes strong enough to survive most weather events.

Likewise, Jesus Christ used the metaphor of a house anchored to a firm foundation when He spoke about having an enduring faith in God.

Therefore, whosoever heareth these sayings of Mine, and doeth them, I will liken him unto a wise man, which built his house upon a rock: And the rain descended, and the floods came, and the winds blew, and beat upon that house; and it fell not: for it was founded upon a rock. (Matthew 7:24–25)

Thus the Lord illustrated the necessity of having a firm biblical foundation for personal redemption.

Furthermore, the Word of God commands parents to pass along biblical values to their children. In a radio message once, I heard a father speak to his son about the most crucial aspect of life, telling him that above all he must get into heaven. As Jesus said,

For what shall it profit a man, if he shall gain the whole world, and lose his own soul? Or what shall a man give in exchange for his soul? (Mark 8:36–37)

This heartfelt plea of a father to his child has stayed with me for over thirty years.

Hence this book is a plea to my children and yours to find the way to heaven. Because what good is wealth and security in this life if you lose your soul in the process? For this reason, I share with you the foundational principles of Christianity that I want to pass on to my family.

After the main text of this book was written, I asked a few of my Christian friends to review it. To my surprise, I discovered that a few of them had objections to the order of the book, for they did not see the need to make biblical knowledge of God's law or the necessity of conviction prerequisites for salvation in Jesus Christ. Therefore, I have added this introduction to remind believers and unbelievers alike that the apostle Paul gives us detailed explanations of each element required for redemption in his epistle to the Romans.

- the authority of God's revelation (chapter 1)
- the sinless nature of God (chapter 1)
- the fallenness and sinfulness of mankind (chapters 2, 3)
- the promised Messiah (chapter 3)
- The purpose of the Law of Moses (chapters 2, 3)
- salvation by grace (chapters 3, 4)
- salvation and justification through faith (chapters 4, 5)
- the purpose of the cross (chapters 3, 4, 5, 6)
- the power of the resurrection (chapter 6)
- the importance of holy living (chapters 7, 8, 12)
- the importance of sharing the gospel (chapters 9, 10, 11)

In this book, I generally follow Paul's method of evangelism, based on God's proper plan of salvation as outlined above. The book is intended to give the average person a clear understanding of the doctrines that each must embrace to secure eternal life and Jesus Christ. May each chapter of my book attach your soul like anchor bolts to the foundation of God's Word and the Savior, Jesus Christ.

The timeless truths found in this volume are nothing new. But they are seldom preached and often dismissed in many modern churches. I have included many quotes from great evangelical saints of the past to buttress my propositions. Thus throughout the book you will see many quotes from some of my favorite Christian authors like the remarkable evangelist and pastor Charles Spurgeon (1834–1892) who prove that each subject below is biblically sound.

Chapter 1

Anchored to Biblical Clarity: Embracing the Confrontational Gospel

*Blows that hurt cleanse away evil, as do
stripes the inner depths of the heart.*
Proverbs 20:30 (NKJV)

Proverbs 20:30 tells us that "blows" (emotionally hurtful confrontation) are necessary for transforming the inward person. Sometimes the truth hurts. But the temporary pain of biblical truth leads to everlasting life. However, in the twenty-first century, many churches have promoted false doctrines about salvation to avoid emotional pain.

Through the ages, false teachers have promised salvation through good works, ceremonial rites, sacraments, church membership, and rituals. Today, more often than not churches falsely promise emotionally painless salvation. They promote eternal deliverance through shallow and simplistic methods that are not authentic, for they eliminate the sound biblical education required to have saving faith in Christ.

The Bible covers difficult emotional subjects. The Word of God deals with the problematic, real-life histories of many people. By reading the Bible, we identify with the victory and heartache of men such as Abraham and David. The God of Abraham, Isaac, and Jacob is a real God who operates in real people's lives and misfortunes. The Bible does not gloss over the trials and the failings inherent in people. God speaks directly to our fallen and sinful human condition by His Word. And the Word of God does not pull its punches, for it aggressively attacks sin and error within each human heart. Likewise, Jesus Christ was often blunt when He spoke to people about the conditions of their sinful hearts. Even a casual reading of the four Gospels reveals how Jesus Christ spoke plainly about the eternal consequences of unbelief and continued rebellion against God:

> If ye continue in My word, then are ye
> My disciples indeed. And ye shall know
> the truth, and the truth shall make you
> free. (John 8:31–32)

However, in our culture, Jesus's example of confrontation is considered crude and impolite. Many churches reject the evangelism methods used by Jesus Christ and His disciples because they fear cultural rejection. But this fear of confrontation always means clarity of thought and sound doctrines are sacrificed on the altars of political correctness and societal sensitivities. Authentic disciples of Christ are never called to sugarcoat or distort biblical truth, for softening the blow of truth destroys clarity and lessens God's extreme importance on eternal salvation.

For greater clarity, Christians need to communicate biblical truth in direct ways that express the urgent need for all people to turn to Christ for genuine salvation. All people need to hear the confrontational truth that leads them to the authentic love, mercy, and forgiveness of God, because sweet-sounding words keep people from taking their eternal fate seriously. As the English preacher Charles Spurgeon said,

> You and I cannot be useful if we want to be sweet as honey in the mouths of men. God will never bless us if we wish to please men, that they may think well of us. Are you willing to tell them what will break your own heart in the telling and break theirs in the hearing? If not, you are not fit to serve the Lord. You must be

willing to go and speak for God, though
you will be rejected. [1]

Spiritual diseases of the heart are akin to physical disorders. A proper diagnosis is necessary to determine a sufficient cure. And like a doctor, the minister of God must determine spiritual maladies and remedies by using the diagnostic tools found within the Word of God. What good is a physician who is unwilling to tell you about a life-threatening but curable cancer because the knowledge of the truth might emotionally upset you? Such a doctor would be guilty of gross negligence and malpractice. Likewise, a minister who tells you that you are loved and that all is well is guilty of malpractice. In reality, he is sending you home to die in your sins. To be saved, we need the emotional maturity to hear the unpleasant truth so that we can have faith in the biblical cure. Charles Spurgeon also said, "Hard words, if they be true, are better than soft words, if they be false."[2]

Nobody can fix spiritual problems in an atmosphere of denial, for we need accurate biblical information to make the right eternal choices. Yet people choose to follow impotent ministers with a sweet bedside manner because they do not want to be challenged

---

[1] Charles Spurgeon, in the sermon "The Message from the Lord's Mouth" (1878).

[2] Charles Spurgeon, in the sermon "The Best Bread" (1847).

emotionally. But scripture warns us to be on guard against these spiritual quacks:

> For the time will come when they will not endure sound doctrine; but after their own lusts, shall they heap to themselves teachers, having itching ears; and they shall turn away their ears from the truth, and shall be turned unto fables. (2 Timothy 4:3–4)

Instead, I challenge you to embrace the complete gospel of Jesus Christ to be saved, which requires conviction, contrition, poverty of spirit, and faith alone in the atoning death and resurrection of Jesus Christ,

Chapter 2

Anchored to Truth

If you wish to know God you must know His word; if you wish to perceive His power you must see how He worketh by His Word.
Charles Spurgeon
"The Swiftly Running Word" (1881)

Absolute truth is knowable and a gift from God. And without reliable truth, it is impossible to be saved or protected from spiritual danger. Thus the Word of God is the indispensable lifeline that all people need to receive to be redeemed. But ignorance of God's Word rejects that lifeline, for God wants us to know Him intimately through His Word and to understand what He has done to save our souls.

Part of knowing God is experiencing Him. But spiritual experiences are not always from God. False spiritual experiences can damage the soul and lead people away from the truth. In the Bible, God has accurately revealed to us everything necessary for a dynamic and redeemed relationship with Him. Therefore, for safety, our relationships with God must be attached to the objective and protective foundation of divine revelation. As Jesus Christ said to the Samaritan woman,

> But the hour cometh, and now is, when the true worshipers shall worship the Father in spirit *and in truth*: For the Father seeketh such to worship Him. God is a Spirit, and they that worship Him must worship Him in spirit *and truth*. (John 4:23–24; emphasis added)

Hence the Lord in His infinite wisdom has revealed to us all the reliable and objective truth required for a safe, intimate, and dynamic relationship with Him.

And so the Word of God is like parents who institute healthy boundaries for their children. When I was a young child, my mother and father gave me rules and guidelines when they sent me out to play. Rule one: stay in the yard. Rule two: do not go into nor play in the street. My parents set physical boundaries that had objective dimensions: the yard was objectively a safer place than the road, where I could be hit by traffic. How I felt about the yard or the street was irrelevant to the set boundaries. I learned from my parents that objective standards and rules from wiser people are beneficial. Later, when I became a Christian, I realized that God had set objective, healthy spiritual standards for all of us. Within these boundaries of truth, safety exists, but outside them, security evaporates.

Furthermore, I found that God's boundaries never hinder authentic worship. Instead, they protect us from deceptive religious experiences and teachings that might lead us astray. Likewise, the apostle Paul proclaimed the necessity of God's boundaries when he wrote,

> All scripture is given by inspiration of God, and is profitable for doctrine, for reproof, for correction, for instruction in righteousness: that the man of God may be perfect, thoroughly furnished unto all good works. (2 Timothy 3:16–17)

Hence, God's Word is directed by the Holy Spirit and is profitable for the complete equipping of God's child. To reject the sufficiency of God's Word is to live without His spiritual protection.

For this reason, reproof and correction must first be made to those who hold a low view of scripture, like those who promote postmodern thinking. Postmodernism is the philosophy that truth is not absolute and is unknowable through any objective means, including reading the Bible. Postmodern Christians promote the idea that somebody can know truth only from within the emotional human spirit. These ministries promote false spiritual experiences to help people find their unique truth, for they think the truth is relative to each person: "your truth is your truth, and my truth is my truth." But if the truth is subjective, how can we be sure of anything? How can personal experience and feelings be the measure of all things? All people make mistakes and get things wrong. So how is it possible for people to find the truth within them? The answer: they cannot.

For the truth to be accurate, it must come from a dependable outside source, and that source must be an all-good, all-knowing God who has revealed it. Postmodernism's core belief is that you cannot trust the Bible to inform about absolute truth. If this premise is correct, there is nothing objectively substantial to base our lives on, and there is nothing outside ourselves that we can trust. But because we are all imperfect, logic dictates that we cannot trust ourselves to find the perfect truth.

Thus the false idea that truth is found within the individual and not objectively in scripture creates a problem for the postmodern or emergent church leader. To maintain the shell of Christianity, the emergent church leader must craft a Jesus that somehow agrees with their experiential, emotional philosophy. Hence they have imagined a Jesus with a different set of morals and standards than the one portrayed in scripture, for they have invented a Jesus consistent with their imagination and feelings. Thus they have made their Jesus more malleable and popular than the authentic Savior revealed in scripture. But the apostle Paul warned us of this kind of distortion when he wrote,

> But I fear, lest by any means, as the serpent beguiled Eve through his subtlety, so your minds should be corrupted from the simplicity that is in Christ, for if he who cometh preacheth another Jesus, whom we have not preached, or if ye receive another spirit, which ye have not received, or another gospel which ye have not accepted, ye might well bear with him. (2 Corinthians 11:3–4)

The central folly of postmodern thinking is that it has no resemblance to the real world. Every day we make thousands of decisions based on the objective reality of the physical world God created. For instance, if you live at the north pole, extreme cold is the reality. But if your feelings tell you it is hot outside, so that you remove your bulky clothing, you will die in the frigid environment. Likewise, mathematics is never subject to relativity. Even if you find the fact

ANCHORED TO THE SAVIOR

emotionally distressing, two plus two always equals four. Also, red traffic signals mean stop. You may feel repressed by that statement, but if you continually run red lights, the objective reality will eventually mean a ticket, an accident, or even death. And no matter your emotional state or philosophical point of view, gravity is always real on earth. Suppose you sincerely believe that your truth defies gravity, and then you jump off a tall building. You will very quickly get educated in the absolute reality of objective fact … just before you hit the pavement. It should be evident that using subjective emotional whims as a means of obtaining truth will lead you to disaster both physically and spiritually.

I minister in prisons regularly. One of the universal truths in prison ministry is that every guilty inmate got themselves into jail when they acted on faulty emotions. They did not adequately consider the consequences of their actions, for most were untrained to operate on biblical principles, and therefore they became slaves to their faulty emotions. Likewise, unless God intervenes, every person left to their false emotions will decay morally because man's natural state is ever-increasing confusion and corruption. Subjectively, people think their heart or feelings will always guide them the right way. But objectively, the Bible tells us the individual emotional heart cannot be trusted and will produce moral corruption. God rebuked the idea that truth is found within the heart when the prophet Jeremiah wrote,

> But they harkened not, nor inclined their ear, but walked in the counsels and in the *imagination* of their evil heart, and went backward, and not forward. (Jeremiah 7:24, emphasis added)

And likewise, God rebuked the subjective wicked heart when He said,

> The heart is deceitful above all things, and desperately wicked: who can know it? (Jeremiah 17:9)

Since your heart deceives you, searching for truth from within will invariably lead you astray from God.

Many people learn the misconception that Christian spirituality is divorced from rationality. This belief is supported by the contemplative prayer movement, which promotes the idea of emptying your rational mind to connect with God. But this is the occult practice of transcendental meditation, which leads people away from the truth by promoting self-centered spirituality. Scripture does not promote the bypassing of the mind or the rejection of objective thought. True biblical meditation ruminates upon the reason and logic of God's Word. God promised a renewed, rational, and sound mind for the redeemed in Jesus Christ. As the apostle Paul writes about the mind in two epistles,

> And be not conformed to this world but be ye transformed by the *renewing of your mind*, that ye may prove what is that good, and acceptable, and perfect, will of God. (Romans 12:2, emphasis added)

And:

> For God hath not given us the spirit of fear, but of power, and of love, and of a *sound mind*. (2 Timothy 1:7, emphasis added)

The false doctrine of bypassing the rational mind is promoted in many churches as part of the Charismatic Movement. But nothing in scripture supports the concept that the Spirit's gifts are alien to or work separately from a logical, rational, and spiritually renewed Christian mind. The opposite is true, as the apostle Paul writes about the gift of prophecy:

> Let two or three prophets speak, and let the others, judge. (1 Corinthians 14:29)

Hence, discernment regarding an utterance's soundness is an activity of the rational, redeemed mind weighing what is said in a church against the Bible's known objective counsel.

We are commanded in scripture not to accept everything we experience in the spiritual-emotional realm, as the apostle John wrote:

> Beloved, believe not every spirit, but try the spirits whether they are of God: because many false prophets are gone out into the world. Hereby know ye the Spirit of God. Every spirit that confesseth that Jesus Christ is come in the flesh is of God, and every spirit that confesseth not that Jesus Christ is come in the flesh is not of God: And this is that spirit of Antichrist. (1 John 4:1–3a)

This criterion is comprehensible to any rational thinker. Anything that contradicts the objective statements found in God's Word emanates from a deceptive spirit and must be rejected.

God especially calls us to use our rational minds as we relate to Him intimately and personally. For as He said,

"Come now, and let us reason together,"
saith the Lord. (Isaiah 1:18a)

So as we learn God's perspective about His nature,
our nature, and the nature of the world, our rational,
renewed mind will find closer intimacy with the Lord.
As Jesus said,

> Thou shalt love the Lord thy God with
> all thy heart, with all thy soul, *and with*
> *all thy mind.* (Matthew 22:37, emphasis
> added)

And so the rational, redeemed mind of a Christian
is a vital spiritual organ, because without thought and
reason based on God's objective Word, it is impossible
to believe in or worship God in truth.

However, trusting in objective biblical boundaries
does not mean we become emotionless in Christ.
Experiencing the authentic power of the Holy Spirit
is very moving. But suppose emotional experiences
and doctrines contradict the objective, rational truth
of God's Word. In that case, we can be sure that those
emotions and ideologies emanate from either a sensual
or a demonic source.

Therefore, we must ask the question, does the
Savior agree with postmodern thought, or does He
refute it? Jesus Christ said,

> If ye continue in My word, then ye are
> My disciples indeed, and *ye shall know*
> *the truth*, and the truth shall make you
> free. (John 8:31–32, emphasis added)

Let us consider this passage at some length. To start, Jesus emphatically declares that His disciples "shall know the truth." Thus any person who does not believe in absolute biblical truth cannot be a true disciple of Christ, for their belief system is contrary to the words of the Lord. As George Burder (1752-1832) wrote, "Whatever contradicts the Word of God should be instantly resisted as diabolical."[3] John 8:31–32 kills any notion that truth is unknowable or has no objective standard, for the Lord proclaimed scripture as the ultimate objective standard. Thus scripture proves that truth resides outside our individual experiences and feelings; therefore, we can be sure the Bible is trustworthy.

Jesus Christ leaves no doubt that belief in His Word's objective reality is a requirement for Christian faith.

> Therefore, whosoever heareth these
> sayings of Mine, and doeth them, I will
> liken him unto a wise man, which built
> his house upon a rock: And the rain

---

[3] George Burder, in Writings of John Bunyan

descended, and the floods came, and the
winds blew, and beat upon that house;
and it fell not: for it was founded upon a
rock. (Matthew 7:24–25)

Jesus Christ equates His teachings to a sure
foundation that the trials and setbacks of life cannot
destroy. Christ's words are like a large, immovable
rock that is secure. Situations may change, emotions
may vary, but the Word of God is always trustworthy,
dependable, and sure. Our Lord has given us all the
substantial truth and evidence we need to be saved
and walk with God. In this way, we discover God's
unique characteristics and attributes within this gift
of scripture.

Chapter 3

Anchored by Scriptural Authority

But, oh, Thou bounteous Giver of all good,
Thou art, of all Thy gifts Thyself thy crown!
William Cowper
"The Morning Walk,"
The Task 5.903

One of the bedrock doctrines of the Old Testament is man's ability to deceive himself. For as the Prophet Jeremiah said,

> The heart is deceitful above all things, and desperately wicked: Who can know it? I the Lord, search the heart, I try the reins, even to give every man according to his ways, and according to the fruits of his doings." (Jeremiah 17:9–10)

And one of the main ways we deceive ourselves is by using our imagination. Imagining new gods and reimagining old pagan gods has become a favorite pastime in the twenty-first century. Look at the medium of film: paganism is on the rise. Movies and comic books make pagan gods into superheroes like Thor or supervillains like Loki. The repackaging of the goddess Diana is the premise of the recent Wonder Woman movies, for limited demigods are all the rage in our society. People want a god that will match their fantasies, and so they create imaginary gods that become their higher power. They tailor their gods by choosing the divine attributes they like best. It is like a Build a God boutique at the local mall. Each bin in this store is labeled with a different divine attribute that a person can choose or reject. They might pick a little love here and some tenderheartedness there, but they avoid the godly traits found in scripture such as absolute holiness, perfect righteousness, or the concept of eternal justice for the wicked dead. These demigods have little resemblance to the God of scripture, and this is all futile, for any god a man can invent is by nature powerless to help him. And most important, a god of your imagination can never save you from your sins.

The Bible commands us to accept the one true and living God: the God who is who He says He is. For God has revealed Himself in detail within the pages of scripture and commands us to believe His definition. To be rewarded with eternal life, we must accept God for who He claims to be. As Hebrews 11:6 states,

> But without faith, it is impossible to please Him, for he that cometh to God must believe that He is, and that He is a rewarder of them that diligently seek Him.

God is who He says He is! God described Himself to Moses when He spoke from the burning bush:

> And Moses said unto God, "Behold, when I come unto the children of Israel, and shall say to them, 'The God of your fathers hath sent me unto you,' and they shall say to me, what is His name?' what shall I say unto them?" And God said unto Moses, "I Am That I Am." And He said, "Thus shalt thou say unto the children of Israel. 'I Am hath sent me unto you." (Exodus 3:13–14)

I Am is the title that indicates God is eternally self-existent, for God is the one true God, the Creator of heaven and earth, and thus human imagination cannot accurately define God. He exists, He describes Himself, and He expects all people to seek His true nature from within His Word.

So within the pages of the Bible, we find the correct characteristics that pertain to God. Subjectively piecing a god together using our defective imagination is folly. For the Lord tells us what He thinks about the evil fantasies of sinners:

> Now therefore go to, speak to the men of Judah, and the inhabitants of Jerusalem, saying, 'Thus saith the Lord; Behold, I frame evil against you., and devise a device against you: Return ye now everyone from his evil way, and make your ways and your doings good.' And they said, There is no hope: But [we] will walk after our own devices, and we will everyone do the *imagination of his evil heart.* (Jeremiah 18:11–12 emphasis added)

Using evil imagination is how rebellious people pick and choose their false gods instead of humbly submitting to the God who has defined Himself. As Charles Spurgeon said, "The worst evils of life are those which do not exist, except in our imagination."[4] Human imagination regresses us spiritually, for it

---

[4] Charles Spurgeon, *"Expositions of the Psalms" in "Sword and the Trowel"*

moves us away from the knowledge of God. As the prophet Jeremiah proclaimed,

> But they hearkened not, nor inclined their ear, but walked in the counsels and in the *imagination* of their evil heart, and went backward, and not forward. (Jeremiah 7:24, emphasis added)

Likewise, God says He hates the wicked imagination of people.

> These six things doth the Lord hate: yea, seven are an abomination unto Him: A proud look, a lying tongue, and hands that shed innocent blood, a heart that *deviseth wicked imaginations.* (Proverbs 6:16–18a, emphasis added)

The apostle Paul credits evil imagination as part of man's readiness to reject the true and living God for polytheistic idolatry.

> For the invisible things of Him from the creation of the world are clearly seen, being understood by the things that are made, even His eternal power and Godhead, so that they are without excuse: Because that, when they knew

God, they glorified Him not as God, neither were thankful; but became vain in their *imaginations*, and their foolish heart was darkened. Professing themselves to be wise, they became fools, and changed the glory of the incorruptible God into an image made like to corruptible man, and to birds, and four-footed beasts, and creeping things. (Romans 1:20–23, emphasis added)

God has warned us through the prophet Jeremiah that wicked imagination can convince us to follow false prophets. And following false prophets bring the hot displeasure of the Lord. For God said,

And the Lord saith, because they have forsaken my law which I set before them, and have not obeyed my voice, neither walked therein; but have walked after the *imagination* of their own heart, and after Baalim, which their fathers taught them: Therefore, thus saith the Lord of hosts, the God of Israel; Behold, I will feed them even this people, with wormwood, and give them water of gall to drink. (Jeremiah 9:13–15, emphasis added)

God further states that false prophets exploit the rebellious imagination of others.

> Thus, saith the Lord of hosts: "Hearken not unto the words of the prophets that prophesy unto you: They make you vain: *They speak a vision of their own heart,* and not out of the mouth of the Lord. They say still unto them that despise Me, the Lord hath said, Ye shall have peace; and they say unto everyone that walketh after the *imagination* of his own heart, no evil shall come upon you. (Jeremiah 23:16–17, emphasis added)

Notice how the false prophets proclaim a wrong message of prosperity and peace to the people, for these frauds echo the corrupt fantasies embedded within those who despise God.

> Furthermore, the apostle Paul warns us against following teachers who cater to our imaginary desires.

> For the time will come when they will not endure sound doctrine; but after their own lusts, shall they heap to themselves teachers, having itching ears; and they shall turn away their ears from the

truth, and shall be turned unto fables. (2 Timothy 4:3–4)

When people shop for the god of their fantasy, they also run after teachers who promote mythologies consistent with their vain imaginations. Therefore, all false doctrine is connected to evil human imagination, and a significant part of Christian witness is disputing these imaginary false doctrines. As the apostle Paul wrote,

> For the weapons of our warfare are not carnal, but mighty through God to the pulling down of strongholds; casting down *imaginations*, and every high thing that exalted itself against the knowledge of God *and bring into captivity every thought to the obedience of Christ.* (2 Corinthians 10:4–5, emphasis added)

Jesus Christ promises that He will deliver us from evil human imagination at His return to Earth. God makes it clear that fantasy has no place in our belief about the Lord. The prophet Jeremiah wrote,

> At that time, they shall call Jerusalem the throne of the Lord; and all the nations shall be gathered unto it, to the name of the Lord, to Jerusalem: neither shall they

walk any more after the *imagination* of
their evil heart. (Jeremiah 3:17, emphasis
added)

However, a redeemed imagination is a beautiful
thing. We can dream up new inventions and create
breathtaking works of art with imagination. But we
do not need to use imagination when it comes to our
relationship with God. God has thoroughly defined
Himself, and these authentic characteristics of the true
and living God are found only in the Christian Bible.
Thus we are called by God to seek Him by faith in His
written revelation.

But without faith, it is impossible to
please Him, for he that cometh to God
must believe that He *is*, and that He is
a rewarder of them that diligently seek
Him. (Hebrews 11:6)

So, then faith cometh by hearing, and
hearing by the word of God. (Romans
10:17)

Only in scripture can we find the genuine attributes
of God. No counterfeit of your imagination will ever
satisfy your desire to know Him.

Chapter 4

Anchored to God's Character

*Who is a God like unto thee, that pardoneth
iniquity, and passeth by the transgression of the
remnant of His heritage? He retaineth not His
anger forever, because He delighteth in mercy.
He will turn again; He will have compassion upon
us; He will subdue our iniquities, and thou wilt
cast all their sins into the depths of the sea.*
Michah 7:18–19

God is a gift to us. A personal relationship with Him is
the ultimate gift, for God wants us to know Him. And
in knowing Him, God wants us to trust in His steadfast
characteristics. Christian worship means recognizing
God's attributes and appreciating His divine features.
Knowing the nature of God is indispensable as it
relates to saving faith. Here are six attributes of God
that are essential to knowing Him.

God Is True

God, through Jeremiah, often compared false prophets to real ones. Lying is a hallmark of false teachers and false prophets because they routinely misrepresent God's will and nature. As God said,

> "For I have not sent them," saith the Lord,
> "Yet they prophesy a lie in My name."
> (Jeremiah 27:15a)

God's written revelation is always true. As the writer of Hebrews explains,

> Wherein God, willing more abundantly to show unto the heirs of promise the immutability of His counsel, confirmed it by an oath: That by two immutable things, in which it was *impossible for God to lie*, we might have a strong consolation, who have fled for refuge to lay hold upon the hope set before us. (Hebrews 6:17–18, emphasis added)

Therefore, we can always trust God to give us the unvarnished truth throughout His Word. The apostle John tells us,

Then cried Jesus in the temple as He
taught, saying, Ye both know Me, and ye
know whence I am: and I am not come
of Myself, *but He that sent me is true,*
whom ye know not. But I know Him:
for I am from Him, and He hath sent me.
(John 7:28–29, emphasis added)

Hence truth is the foundational attribute of God
upon which all His other qualities rest. Without truth,
it is impossible to know anything about the character
of God. For truth defines the Creator. Truth defines sin.
Truth defines love. And truth defines God's merciful
salvation, for God personifies truth.

God Is Creator

The Bible begins with a single premise:

In the beginning, God created the heaven
and the earth. (Genesis 1:1)

The Gospel of John begins with the same premise:

In the beginning was the Word, and the
Word was with God, and the Word was
God. The same was in the beginning with
God. All things were made by Him; and
without Him was not anything made that

was made. In Him was life; and the life was the light of men. (John 1:1–4)

Therefore, God—Father, Son, and Holy Spirit—made all material things. God is the first un-caused cause of all creation. As the psalmist declared,

The heavens are Thine; the earth also is Thine: as for the world and the fullness thereof, Thou hast founded them. (Psalm 89:11)

As Creator, God owns everything and has the right to exercise authority over it. God the Creator has the right to make all the rules by which humanity must live. He is Lord of all. As the Word says,

The earth is the LORD's, and the fullness thereof; the world, and they that dwell therein. (Psalm 24:1)

So God expects all people to surrender to His Lordship and obey His rules. Anything less than total obedience is sin.

God Is Omnipresent

The pagan concept of the divine is a multitude of finite gods, all hampered by time and space. Hence location and purpose limit these so-called gods that demand the worship of idols. But the apostle Paul said,

> The things which the Gentiles sacrifice, they sacrifice to devils, and not to God: and I would not that ye should have fellowship with devils. (1 Corinthians 10:20)

Paul confirms that pagan gods are nothing more than demonic counterfeits of the one true and living God. Unlike the counterfeits, the God of scripture has no physical limitations, for He exists everywhere.

Jonah thought he could get away from the influence of God by leaving the territory of Israel. But Jonah found out you can never get away from the authentic God. No matter how far Jonah traveled, he couldn't run away from God, for God is always near to His creation.

Knowing that God is always near is an excellent gift to the believer, for the nearness of God is a great comfort to those who put their trust in Him. As King David explained,

> Whither shall I go from Thy Spirit? or whither shall I flee from Thy presence? If I ascend up into heaven, Thou art there: if I make my bed in hell, behold, Thou art

there. If I take the wings of the morning,
and dwell in the uttermost parts of the
sea; Even there shall Thy hand lead me,
and Thy right hand shall hold me. (Psalm
139:7–10)

God is never far away. He is as close as a prayer.

God Is Eternal

The reason we can always trust in the good gifts of
God is that God will never cease to exist. For the Word
says,

And Abraham planted a grove in
Beersheba, and called there on the
name of the LORD, the *everlasting God.*
(Genesis 21:33 emphasis added)

And Moses spoke of God's eternal nature in a
psalm attributed to him:

Before the mountains were brought forth,
or ever thou hadst formed the earth and
the world, even from everlasting to
everlasting, Thou art God. (Psalm 90:2a)

Isaiah described God as "the high and lofty One
that inhabiteth eternity" (Isaiah 57:15). Eternal life

can be found only within the power and purpose of an eternal God.

God Is Omnipotent

God needs more than a desire to save us. God must also have the power to save, for salvation requires God's omnipotent ability to regenerate each human soul. And for God to renew a soul, He must have the power to create.

Scripture reveals to us that God is the all-powerful Creator, and so God can do all things consistent with His good and perfect will. Likewise, when Jesus walked the earth, He proved His divine nature by working many omnipotent miracles. Jesus healed the sick, walked on water, calmed the sea, and raised the dead. Jesus did these wonders to prove that He is the God of creation.

Salvation requires faith in a miracle-working God. Nothing is too difficult for Him. As the Word says,

> Ah Lord GOD! behold, Thou hast made the heaven and the earth by thy great power and stretched out arm, and there is nothing too hard for Thee. (Jeremiah 32:17)

God Is Good and Not the Author of Evil

God alone has the holiness, knowledge, and authority to determine good from evil. Genesis 1:31 proclaims that God made all things good, for God is good by nature. Therefore, the existence of evil must be a degradation or perversion of that good initial creation. As the apostle James proclaimed,

> Every good gift and every perfect gift is from above, and cometh down from the Father of lights, with Whom is no variableness, neither shadow of turning. (James 1:17)

Therefore, when Satan and later Adam and Eve fell into sin, they perverted what God had made. In love, God gave them the free will to love Him in obedience or reject Him by sin. When they chose to sin, the shadow of evil fell upon all creation (Genesis 3). Evil was invented by Satan and man, not by God.

Chapter 5

Anchored to God's Character, Continued

O for a thousand tongues to sing my great Redeemer's praise, the glories of my God and King, the triumphs of His grace!
Charles Wesley (1707–1788)

We often hear people say, "Why can't you accept me for who I am?" I must have said this to my parents a hundred times to justify my poor school performance and slothful teenage rebellion. But now I see how emotionally manipulative that statement is. And many people try to manipulate God the same way. They try to justify their rebellion against Him when they say, "God, if you love me, you will always accept me just as I am, sin and warts and all." But this kind of thinking is at odds with the character of God. In an effort to change God's perfect righteousness and to degrade God's character to their level. They want His

REV. PATRICK EDWIN HARRIS

standards of holiness adapted to their sinful ways. But as Lord of Heaven and Earth, God requires us to accept *Him* for who He is. Salvation has us adapting to God's standards through the process of redemption, and not the other way around. Learning about God's perfect character and attributes is a vital part of this necessary transformation.

God Is Holy

As the psalmist said,

> The LORD *is* righteous in all His ways,
> and holy in all His works. (Psalm 145:17)

The existence of evil and sin does not change the excellent character of God, for the shadow of sin only brings more distinction to the light of His goodness and holiness.

Holiness is the idea that God is entirely separate from evil and sin, for God is always just and moral. He is permanently distinct from all injustice and immorality. God alone can make absolute moral distinctions. If God were to condone even the slightest sin, God would no longer be good or holy. Even the most minor sin drives an eternal wedge between God and us, and so Adam and Eve were removed from the sacred presence of God. They were cast out of the garden of Eden because of their rebellion and sin.

God Is Omniscient

God knows it all. He knows every deed you have ever done. He knows every evil fantasy of your mind. He knows all the secrets of your past. He knows the anger and bitterness that consume you. He knows all the unforgiveness in your heart. And He knows all your lame excuses and rationalizations for continuing to sin. He knows every curse of your lips. God knows every sin that you have ever committed

However, God also knows every good deed you have attempted. He knows every wounding of your soul. He is aware of every hurt you have suffered. And He knows all the injustice you have received because God knows all things.

Therefore, God knows you at your best, and God knows you at your worst. As the apostle John wrote,

> For if our heart condemns us, God is greater than our heart, and knoweth all things. (1 John 3:20)

And yet, even though God knows all of your moral failures, inexplicably this Holy God still wants to redeem you.

God Is Immutable

Immutability means that God does not change. God said, "I am the LORD, I change not" (Malachi 3:6a). The God who condemned the world and brought judgment by a flood is the same God who will bring ultimate judgment by fire at the end of the age, as predicted by the apostle Peter.

> Whereby the world that then was, being overflowed with water, perished: But the heavens and the earth, which are now, by the same word are kept in store, reserved unto fire against the day of judgment and perdition of ungodly men. (2 Peter 3:6–7)

Thus the God who saved Noah and his family by His mercy and grace will likewise save believers in Christ by His mercy and grace. The same Jesus Christ who came as a merciful savior during His first advent will one day bring judgment at His second advent.

Therefore, in every age, the gospel is the same, and those who refuse to receive Christ's mercy will instead receive Christ's judgment. Because "Jesus Christ [is] the same yesterday, and today, and forever" (Hebrews 13:8), our faith must be anchored to God's unchanging nature.

God Is the Righteous Judge

Since God alone determines right from wrong, God alone is the ultimate righteous judge. For the psalmist said,

> Righteous *art* thou, O LORD, and upright *are* thy judgments. (Psalm 119:137)

God judges all sinners who violate His perfect will:

> I the LORD search the heart, I try the reins, even to give every man according to his ways, and according to the fruit of his doings. (Jeremiah 17:10)

God warned Adam and Eve that judgment would come upon them if they rebelled against His statutes.

> And the LORD God took the man and put him into the garden of Eden to dress it and to keep it. And the LORD God commanded the man, saying, Of every tree of the garden thou mayest freely eat: But of the tree of the knowledge of good and evil, thou shalt not eat of it: for in the day that thou eatest thereof thou shalt surely die. (Genesis 2:15–17)

Once they rebelled, Adam and Eve died spiritually and were disconnected from the life-giving power of God. And without this spiritual power, their bodies eventually wore out, and they ultimately died physically. Therefore, spiritual and physical death is God's righteous judgment on humanity. As the apostle Paul said, "The wages of sin is death" (Romans 6:23a).

God will judge all humanity at the end of time.

> And I saw a great white throne, and Him that sat on it, from whose face the earth and the heaven fled away; and there was found no place for them. And I saw the dead, small, and great, stand before God; and the books were opened: and another book was opened, which is the book of life: and the dead were judged out of those things which were written in the books, according to their works. (Revelation 20:12)

God Is Merciful

Even though we must all pass through the righteous judgment of God, we have the consolation that God is merciful. God maintained His people Israel with mercy, even during their rebellion. As Nehemiah said,

But they and our fathers dealt proudly, and hardened their necks, and hearkened not to Thy commandments, and refused to obey, neither were mindful of Thy wonders that Thou didst among them; but hardened their necks, and in their rebellion appointed a captain to return to their bondage: *but Thou art a God ready to pardon, gracious and merciful, slow to anger, and of great kindness, and forsook them not.*" (Nehemiah 9:16-17 emphasis added)

Hence, even though God must judge our sin, God also wants to give us mercy. For the righteous God is also long-suffering and merciful. His goodness is like a coin: on one side of the coin, this righteous God must judge and punish sin, But on the other side, this merciful God desires to forgive and pardon the guilty sinner.

In His mercy, God did not slay Adam and Eve instantly when they sinned. Instead, by His mercy He gave them hope for redemption, for He promised them a future savior born of a woman's seed. And from the beginning (Genesis 3:15), God predicted the merciful hope of a coming messiah, Jesus Christ. Moreover, by His mercy, in Genesis 3:21 God hid their shame by covering their nakedness with the skins of animals, which symbolized Christ's ultimate sacrifice to cover our sin.

God Is Savior

God promised salvation to Adam and Eve through faith in a future savior, for God is the Savior of His people. As the Word says,

> The LORD is my light and my salvation; whom shall I fear? the LORD is the strength of my life; of whom shall I be afraid? (Psalm 27:1)

Therefore, Jesus Christ came to save sinners by reconciling them to God the Father. And this process of spiritual reconciliation is called redemption.

The concept of "savior" is one who rescues you from a destructive fate that you have no power to control. Just as a drowning child needs a lifeguard to save them, so too a sinner drowning in iniquity needs a saving God.

My great uncle was a sailor on the USS *Indianapolis* at the end of World War II. One day, Uncle Ralph found himself in the ocean after a torpedo sank the ship. He and the other survivors spent many days in the sea without food or drinking water. And to make matters worse, they were surrounded by sharks. Many of the original survivors were killed and eaten by sharks. For the remaining few, the only chance of survival was saving intervention by others. In the end, Uncle Ralph and the remaining sailors were spotted by plane crews and saved from imminent death.

Spiritually, all sinners are in a similar situation, for we are drowning in a sea of sinfulness and have no way to rescue ourselves. We need God to save and deliver us from this sea of sin and despair. Without God's intervention, we are in a hopeless situation. Hence God sent His Son, Jesus Christ, to rescue us. As the Word says,

> Him hath God exalted with his right hand to be a Prince and a Saviour, for to give repentance to Israel, and forgiveness of sins. (Acts 5:31)

God so loved this world of shipwrecked sinners that He sent a Savior, Jesus Christ.

God Is Love

God, by nature, is a loving God, for God deeply cares about people and their eternal well-being. Since God is love, He must define love, and thus He is our example of how to love others. Furthermore, He offers sinners forgiveness of sin and salvation by His love. For the apostle John wrote,

> In this was manifested the love of God toward us because God sent His only begotten Son into the world, that we might live through Him. Herein is love, not that we loved God, but that He loved us, and sent His Son to be the propitiation for our sins. (1 John 4:9–10)

The ultimate example of love is what Jesus Christ did on the cross to atone for our sins. God's love is a selfless act of benevolence that benefits undeserving believers.

Moreover, this act of benevolence required Christ to suffer loss, pain, and death—an act of selfless love or charity, the term used in the King James Version Bible to describe Christ's perfect love.

> Though I speak with the tongues of men and of angels, and have not charity, I am become *as* sounding brass, or a tinkling cymbal. And though I have *the gift of* prophecy, and understand all mysteries, and all knowledge; and though I have all faith, so that I could remove mountains, and have not charity, I am nothing. And

though I bestow all my goods to feed the poor, and though I give my body to be burned, and have not charity, it profiteth me nothing. Charity suffereth long and is kind; charity envieth not; charity vaunteth not itself, is not puffed up, Doth not behave itself unseemly, seeketh not her own, is not easily provoked, thinketh no evil; Rejoiceth not in iniquity, but rejoiceth in the truth. Beareth all things, believeth all things, hopeth all things, endureth all things. Charity never faileth. (1 Corinthians 13:1–8a)

God's kind of love is a willingness to sacrifice for the well-being of others, for charity has pity and compassion for the plight of others, regardless of their unworthiness. Charitable love is based purely on the other person's need. It is the selfless compassion expressed in the Greek language as *agape* love, charity to the undeserving. As the apostle John said,

For God so loved the world, that He gave His only begotten Son, that whosoever believeth in Him should not perish, but have everlasting life. (John 3:16)

God has such pity and compassion for undeserving sinners that He sent His own Son to sacrifice His life for them as an act of cosmic charity.

To experience God's love, we must understand that certain conditions must be met. First, we are called to humble ourselves and believe that Jesus Christ bore the punishment for our sins on the cross. Second, we must believe that Jesus Christ has fulfilled all conditions required that allow us to have a loving relationship with God the Father. And finally, our souls must be reconnected to God through spiritual regeneration.

Chapter 6

Anchored to the Promised Messiah

*Come, thou long-expected Jesus, born to
set thy people free; from our fears and sins
release us; let us find our rest in thee.*
Charles Wesley

*If Christ is not all to you He is nothing to you. He
will never go into partnership as a part Saviour of
men. If He be something He must be everything,
and if He be not everything He is nothing to you.*
Charles Spurgeon
"Christ is All" (1871)

The ultimate gift of God is the Savior, Jesus Christ.
He alone gives meaning to life. To have everything
without Christ is nothing, and to have nothing except
Christ is everything, because riches and health can
disappear in the blink of an eye, and nothing in this life

is permanent. But authentic salvation grants eternal life to the believer in Jesus Christ. Jesus Christ is the ultimate gift that "will never leave thee, nor forsake thee" (Hebrews 13:5).

However, God needs to combat all false religious ideas that corrupt and hinder salvational faith to fulfill His plan for redemption. And so God challenged false pagan ideology by choosing a man named Abraham to create a new pagan-free nation that would serve and worship Him alone. Moreover, by this chosen nation, God would compile His complete Bible. Therefore, through Israel, God's absolute truth was collected and safeguarded for the entire world to receive. Furthermore, within this nation of Israel, God would send His Son, the Messiah, to conquer sin and death.

God sent prophets to Israel to declare His Word and predict the Messiah's coming. Understanding fulfilled prophecy strengthens our faith and anchors us to the present messiah. By these prophecies, God foretold the Messiah's future life, work, death on a cross, and resurrection. Hence many Old Testament prophecies are the cosmic address for the one true Messiah, Jesus Christ. This cosmic address is so precise and detailed that only Jesus Christ can be that person. To get mail requires only five markers: your name, street number, street name, city, and state. But to identify the one true Messiah, God gave us hundreds of predictive markers that allows us to recognize Him. Since Jesus Christ is the only person in human history that matches all these prophetic clues, we can be sure that He is the one true Messiah.

For example, Isaiah prophesied about many of these Messianic indicators:

> Therefore, the Lord himself shall give you a sign; Behold, a virgin shall conceive, and bear a Son, and shall call His name Immanuel [God with us]. (Isaiah 7:14)

> For unto us a Child is born, unto us a Son is given, and the government shall be upon His shoulder: and His name shall be called Wonderful, Counselor, The Mighty God, The everlasting Father, The Prince of Peace. (Isaiah 9:6)

These prophecies of Isaiah were reaffirmed by the angel Gabriel, as Luke's Gospel says:

> And in the sixth month the angel Gabriel was sent from God unto a city of Galilee, named Nazareth, to a virgin espoused to a man whose name was Joseph, of the house of David; and the virgin's name was Mary. And the angel came in unto her, and said, Hail, thou that art highly favored, the Lord is with thee: blessed art

thou among women. And when she saw him, she was troubled at his saying, and cast in her mind what manner of salutation this should be. And the angel said unto her, Fear not, Mary: for thou hast found favor with God. And behold, thou shalt conceive in thy womb, and bring forth a Son, and shalt call His name JESUS. He shall be great and shall be called the Son of the Highest: and the Lord God shall give unto Him the throne of his father David: And He shall reign over the house of Jacob forever; and of His kingdom, there shall be no end. Then said Mary unto the angel, how shall this be, seeing I know not a man? And the angel answered and said unto her, The Holy Ghost shall come upon thee, and the power of the Highest shall overshadow thee: therefore, also that holy [One] which shall be born of thee shall be called the Son of God. (Luke 1:26–35)

In the book of Matthew, we read the account of how Isaiah's prophecies are fulfilled:

Now the birth of Jesus Christ was on this wise: When as His mother Mary was espoused to Joseph, before they came together, she was found with child of the Holy Ghost. Then Joseph, her husband, being a just man, and not willing to make her a public example, was minded putting her away privily. But while he thought on these things, behold, the angel of the Lord appeared unto him in a dream, saying, Joseph, thou son of David, fear not to take unto thee Mary thy wife: for that which is conceived in her is of the Holy Ghost. And she shall bring forth a Son, and thou shalt call His name JESUS: for He shall save His people from their sins. Now all this was done, that it might be fulfilled which was spoken of the Lord by the prophet, saying, Behold, a virgin shall be with child, and shall bring forth a Son, and they shall call His name Emmanuel, which being interpreted is, God with us. (Matthew 1:18–23)

After the birth of Christ, the fulfillment of these prophecies was confirmed by the holy angels. Luke tells us,

And there were in the same country shepherds abiding in the field, keeping watch over their flock by night. And, lo, the angel of the Lord came upon them, and the glory of the Lord shone round about them: and they were sore afraid. And the angel said unto them, Fear not: for, behold, I bring you good tidings of great joy, which shall be to all people. For unto you is born this day in the city of David a Savior, which is Christ the Lord. And this shall be a sign unto you; Ye shall find the Babe wrapped in swaddling clothes, lying in a manger. (Luke 2:8–12)

Furthermore, God used Old Testament prophecy to predict the unique death of Jesus Christ. Scripture describes our Lord's terrible humiliation on the cross in Psalm 22. Remember, this prophecy existed hundreds of years before the Romans employed crucifixion. About a thousand years before Christ's death, King David wrote this prophecy:

"My God, my God, why hast thou forsaken Me? Why art thou so far from helping Me, and from the words of My roaring? O my God, I cry in the daytime, but thou hearest not; and in the night season and am not silent. But thou art holy, O thou that inhabitest the praises of Israel. Our fathers trusted in thee: they trusted, and thou didst deliver them. They cried unto thee, and were delivered: they trusted in thee, and were not confounded. But I am a worm, and no man; a reproach of men, and despised of the people. All they that see Me laugh me to scorn, they shoot out the lip, they shake the head, saying, He trusted on the LORD that He would deliver Him: let Him deliver Him, seeing He delighted in him. But thou art He that took me out of the womb: thou didst make Me hope when I was upon My mother's breasts. I was cast upon Thee from the womb: thou art my God from my mother's belly. Be not far from Me; for trouble is near; for there is none to help. Many bulls have compassed Me: strong bulls of Bashan have beset Me round. They gaped upon Me with their mouths, as a ravening and a roaring lion. I am poured out like water, and all My bones are out of joint: My heart is like wax; it is melted in the midst of My bowels. My strength is dried up like a potsherd; and My tongue cleaveth to my jaws; and thou hast brought Me into the dust of death. For dogs have compassed

Me: the assembly of the wicked have
enclosed Me: they pierced My hands and
My feet. I may tell all my bones: they
look and stare upon Me. They part My
garments among them and cast lots upon
My vesture. (Psalm 22:1–18)

Psalm 22 proves the veracity of Jesus's claim to
be the one true Messiah. Note the gruesome details
of Christ's crucifixion. The physical condition of a
crucified man. The piercing of the hands and feet by
Gentiles. The gambling for the clothes of the Lord.
The mocking and rejection by the religious leaders.
And the words that Jesus Christ would quote on the
cross: "My God, My God, why hast Thou forsaken
Me?" With that statement, He declared that He was
the one and only suffering Messiah predicted by King
David.

Matthew records the fulfillment of Psalm 22:

And they crucified Him, and parted
His garments, casting lots: that it might
be fulfilled which was spoken by the
prophet, they parted My garments among
them, and upon My vesture did they cast
lots. And sitting down they watched
him there; And set up over His head His
accusation written, THIS IS JESUS THE

KING OF THE JEWS. Then were there two thieves crucified with Him, one on the right hand, and another on the left. And they that passed by reviled Him, wagging their heads, and saying, Thou that destroyest the temple, and buildest *it* in three days, save Thyself. If Thou be the Son of God, come down from the cross. Likewise, also the chief priests mocking Him, with the scribes and elders, said, He saved others; Himself he cannot save. If He be the King of Israel, let Him now come down from the cross, and we will believe Him. He trusted in God; let Him deliver Him now, if he will have Him: for he said, I am the Son of God ... Now from the sixth hour there was darkness over all the land unto the ninth hour. And about the ninth hour Jesus cried with a loud voice, saying, Eli, Eli, lama sabachthani? that is to say, My God, my God, why hast thou forsaken Me? (Matthew 27:35–46)

John the Baptist had recognized Jesus Christ as the predicted Messiah. John indicates the sacrifice of Jesus on the cross by calling Him the Lamb of God.

The next day John seeth Jesus coming unto him, and saith, Behold the Lamb of God, which taketh away the sin of the world. This is He of whom I said, after me cometh a man which is preferred before me: for He was before me. (John 1:29–30)

In conclusion, all the Old Testament predictive indicators point to one person as the coming messiah, Jesus Christ. Around a hundred of these predictions were fulfilled by Jesus Christ. Old Testament prophecy is so accurate that even the exact year of Jesus's death was predicted for AD 30 by Daniel the prophet. Therefore, no other person but Jesus Christ can claim to be the legitimate promised Messiah.

Chapter 7

Anchored by Mosaic Law

*The first duty of the gospel preacher is to declare
God's law and to show the nature of sin.*
Martin Luther

*It is not God's way to make men alive, again,
until they are really dead, I mean that,
spiritually, they must be first slain by the law
before they are made alive by the Gospel.*
Charles Spurgeon,
"Hope for the Worst Backsliders"

For more than sixty years, many myths about salvation
have dominated evangelical churches. One of these
myths is that people automatically know they are
sinners and are filled with shame about their sin. Many
ministers believe this fable and refuse to preach on sin
and repentance—they want only to encourage people,
and so they refuse to teach the whole counsel of God.

To the shallow minister and congregation, sin is a downer that must be avoided in order to attract a large congregation. Consequently, these ministries boil down the evangelical message to a single magical prayer that goes something like "Lord Jesus come into my life" or "Lord Jesus come into my heart." And then the arrogant minister assures anyone who prays these prayers that they are saved. How quick, simple, and easy! No conviction or contrition is required. No changing your mind is necessary. There is no requirement to understand God's plan of salvation, and no need to prepare your soul to be saved. Just speak a magic incantation without thought or faith, and you are part of the Kingdom of God.

But this kind of shallow thinking is unbiblical and has no power to save souls. Many have fallen away from Christianity because they never understood or received the authentic Gospel, And therefore they were never authentically redeemed by the Holy Spirit. there is nothing sadder than an unregenerate person who falsely assumes they are going to heaven. These misguided people never see their need for divine forgiveness or salvation. Jesus Christ said of this kind of person:

> Not everyone that saith unto me, Lord, Lord, shall enter into the kingdom of heaven; but he that doeth the will of my

ANCHORED TO THE SAVIOR

Father which is in heaven. Many will say
to Me in that day, Lord, Lord, have we
not prophesied in Thy name? And in Thy
name have cast out devils? And in Thy
name done many wonderful works? And
then will I profess unto them, I never
knew you: depart from Me, ye that work
iniquity. (Matthew 7:21–23)

Notice how this person trusts an assumed salvation,
for they base their entrance into the kingdom of God
on religious performance. See also how they brag to
Jesus Christ about what they have done for God. In
their minds, God is obligated to accept them based on
their good deeds. And if we apply this scripture to our
modern era, it will sound something like this: "Lord,
did we not say the magic saving prayer? Did we not
go to church from time to time? Did we not become
members of the correct religious organization? Did
we not give money to a good cause? And did we not
follow and support the right minister?"

But Christ's message is clear: the false believer
trusts in what they have done for God instead of on
what God has done for them. Their pride keeps them
from true salvation. Thus the shallow believer never
allows the Law of Moses to humble them and prepare
them to meet the Savior.

Preparation of the soul is indispensable to genuine

salvation. God sent John the Baptist to prepare people to meet Jesus Christ, and John the Baptist used the Law of Moses to do this work. John called all people to change their minds and to agree with God that they were sinners who routinely violated Mosaic law. The Gospel of Mark says,

> The beginning of the gospel of Jesus Christ, the Son of God; As it is written in the prophets, Behold, I send My messenger before thy face, which shall prepare thy way before thee. The voice of one crying in the wilderness, prepare ye the way of the Lord, make His paths straight. John did baptize in the wilderness and preach the baptism of repentance for the remission of sins. And there went out unto him all the land of Judea, and they of Jerusalem, and were all baptized of him in the river of Jordan, confessing their sins. And John was clothed with camel's hair, and with a girdle of a skin about his loins; and he did eat locusts and wild honey; And preached, saying, "There cometh One mightier than I after me, the latches of Whose shoes I am not worthy to stoop down and unloose. I indeed have baptized you with water:

but He shall baptize you with the Holy Ghost." (Mark 1:1–8)

The ministry of confession and repentance is the soul's preparation making our path straight so Jesus Christ can save us, for confession and repentance are indispensable aspects of true salvation. Confession of sin requires individuals to have sufficient knowledge of the concept of sin, while ignorance of sin hinders repentance.

The word "repentance" means simply changing your mind when God calls you to give up your way of thinking and agree with Him about His perspective on your sinful situation. John the Baptist called on everyone to agree with God that they had fallen short of God's legal standard and that without forgiveness from God they would never receive eternal life. The baptism of John was an outward symbol of the inward preparation of the mind and soul. This preparation acknowledges personal iniquity and the need for divine forgiveness.

John the Baptist's popularity was enabled by the fact that the Israelites were educated in the Law of Moses and therefore deeply understood the concept of personal sin. The law's purpose was not to save people but rather to educate them about their fallenness and hence understand their need for miraculous salvation.

At the beginning of His ministry, Jesus Christ too preached the need to repent based on Mosaic law.

> Think not that I am come to destroy the law, or the prophets: I am not come to destroy, but to fulfill. For verily I say unto you, till heaven and earth pass, one jot or one tittle shall in no wise pass from the law, till all be fulfilled. Whosoever therefore shall break one of these least commandments, and shall teach men so, he shall be called the least in the Kingdom of Heaven: but whosoever shall do and teach them, the same shall be called great in the Kingdom of Heaven. (Matthew 5:17-19)

Furthermore, Jesus took the radical step of applying the law of Moses to thoughts and not just actions.

> Ye have heard that it was said by them of old time, Thou shalt not kill; and whosoever shall kill shall be in danger of the judgment: But I say unto you, That whosoever is angry with his brother without a cause shall be in danger of the judgment: and whosoever shall say to his brother, Raca, shall be in danger of the

council: but whosoever shall say, Thou fool, shall be in danger of hell fire ... Ye have heard that it was said by them of old time, Thou shalt not commit adultery: But I say unto you, That whosoever looketh on a woman to lust after her hath committed adultery with her already in his heart. (Matthew 5:21–22, 27–28)

Thus Jesus Christ made total compliance with the Mosaic law the standard of righteousness. God judges every thought and attitude of the heart, and by this standard, no one can claim to have enough righteousness to enter heaven, for no honest person can claim that every thought and action since birth has been in harmony with God.

Mosaic law gloriously reveals God's perfect righteous character, compares Christ's character against the sinful nature of every human being, and hence shows all men their need for divine forgiveness and salvation. God's law is fulfilled when it exposes the wickedness of every human heart. For the Lord said,

The heart is deceitful above all things, and desperately wicked: who can know it? I the LORD search the heart, I try the reins, even to give every man according to his ways, and according to the fruit of his doings. (Jeremiah 17:9–10)

Jesus Christ also made the fallen condition of the heart clear, prompted by Peter's desire to know more about it, saying,

> Not that which goeth into the mouth defileth a man; but that which cometh out of the mouth, this defileth a man... Then answered Peter and said unto him, Declare unto us this parable. And Jesus said, Are ye also yet without understanding? Do not ye yet understand, that whatsoever entereth in at the mouth goeth into the belly, and is cast out into the draught? But those things which proceed out of the mouth come forth from the heart; and they defile the man. *For out of the heart proceed evil thoughts, murders, adulteries, fornications, thefts, false witness, blasphemies: These are the things which defile a man:* but to eat with unwashed hands defileth not a man. (Matthew 15:11, 15-20 emphasis added)

Our Lord applies the law of Moses to every human heart's internal workings and declares them unworthy.

The law rightly applied exposes the corrupt nature of each person. Likewise, the apostle Paul taught that the law prepares the heart for genuine salvation.

> Now we know that what things soever the law saith, it saith to them who are under the law: that every mouth may be stopped, *and all the world may become guilty before God. Therefore, by the deeds of the law there shall no flesh be justified in His sight: for by the law is the knowledge of sin.* (Romans 3:19–20, emphasis added)

> Wherefore then serveth the law? It was added because of transgressions ... Is the law then against the promises of God? God forbid, for if there had been a law given which could have given life, verily righteousness should have been by the law. *But the scripture hath concluded all under sin,* that the promise by faith of Jesus Christ might be given to them that believe. But before faith came, we were kept under the law, shut up unto the faith which should afterwards be revealed. Wherefore the law was our schoolmaster to bring us unto Christ, that we might

be justified by faith. (Galatians 3:19–24
emphasis added)

Mosaic law is fulfilled when our self-righteous bragging ends, we acknowledge our guilt before God, and we admit we are sinners rightly condemned by a just God, for the law was never meant to make us worthy of heaven. But instead, by the law, we discover that we will never be worthy of heaven on our own. To enter heaven, we need God's merciful intervention. The law prepares us to accept that we are helpless sinners in desperate need of a Savior.

Chapter 8

Anchored by Conviction

The recognition of sin is the beginning of salvation.
Martin Luther

The fear of the Lord is a fountain of life,
to depart from the snares of death.
Proverbs 14:27

Conviction is a beautiful gift from God, for without deep conviction of sin, it is impossible to fear God's judgment or to see our need for deliverance and salvation. It is good news that God has not abandoned us to figure this out for ourselves. Instead, conviction is a supernatural work of the Holy Spirit.

In the previous chapter, we saw that God's law was given to us to recognize our sinful state logically and rationally. The Law of Moses is the objective standard of truth that convinces our minds about sin. Moreover, in addition to the law, Jesus Christ promised to send the Holy Spirit to confront us about sin and comfort us with forgiveness when we repent. The direct experiential witness of the Holy Spirit that reproves our sin was ordained by Jesus Christ when He said,

> Nevertheless, I tell you the truth; It is expedient for you that I go away: for if I go not away, the Comforter will not come unto you; but if I depart, I will send Him unto you. And when He is come, He will reprove the world of sin, and of righteousness, and of judgment. (John 16:7–8)

The Holy Spirit's mission therefore is to personally reprove all unsaved people about their sinfulness in unity with the Law of Moses and thus to bear witness to each soul of their need for Jesus Christ to save and forgive them. This work of conviction works best when the Bible is proclaimed to the hearts and minds of sinners. As the apostle Peter said,

> Knowing this first, that no prophecy of the scripture is of any private interpretation. For prophecy came not in old time by the will of man: but holy men of God spake as they were moved by the Holy Ghost. (2 Peter 1:20–21)

Sometimes the word translated as "prophecy" in scripture refers to telling the future. But in this context, Peter means prophecy as the accurate pronouncement of God's thoughts and perspectives. Therefore, since the Holy Spirit is the ultimate author of scripture, His convicting power will always be consistent with the Bible. In other words, the experience of spiritual conviction is always synced to the authoritative proclamation of God's law. Thus, God brings conviction to souls when the Word of God is preached entirely and accurately, as the apostle Paul said,

> For after that in the wisdom of God the world by wisdom knew not God, it pleased God by the foolishness of preaching to save them that believe. (1 Corinthians 1:21)

And so when a person falls under conviction of sin by the power of the Holy Spirit, they recognize their eternal condemnation. But they also become aware that Jesus Christ is the answer to this problem of sin, and so Holy Spirit conviction also brings the hope of deliverance to the humble.

However, it is a common myth in religious circles that condemnation happens only at the end of time when God judges the living and the dead. But Jesus renounces this error in the Gospel of John:

> God sent not his Son into the world to
> condemn the world; but that the world
> through Him might be saved. He that
> believeth on Him is not condemned:
> *but he that believeth not is condemned*
> *already,* because he hath not believed in
> the name of the only begotten Son of God.
> And this is the condemnation, that light
> is come into the world, and men loved
> darkness rather than light, because their
> deeds were evil. (John 3:17–19, emphasis
> added)

The word "world" dictated by the context of the passage means the totality of all humanity. Jesus did not come to condemn people, because eternal condemnation is preset. As the scriptures proclaim, "For all have sinned and fall short of the glory of God" (Romans 3:23). The only way out of this preset damnation is deliverance by Jesus Christ, and *the mission of Jesus Christ is to rescue the damned.* But damnation is temporarily suspended by God's mercy while we are physically alive; that is, God suspends the execution of His judgment so we can turn to Jesus Christ for deliverance. As the apostle Peter says,

> The Lord is not slack concerning his
> promise, as some men count slackness;

but is longsuffering toward us, not willing that any should perish, but that all should come to repentance. (2 Peter 3:9)

All people can be described as convicted sinners in need of divine deliverance in God's eyes. The apostle Paul wrote,

> As it is written, There is none righteous, no, not one: There is none that understandeth, there is none that seeketh after God. They are all gone out of the way, they are together become unprofitable; there is none that doeth good, no, not one. Their throat is an open sepulchre; with their tongues they have used deceit; the poison of asps is under their lips: Whose mouth is full of cursing and bitterness: Their feet are swift to shed blood: Destruction and misery are in their ways: And the way of peace have they not known: There is no fear of God before their eyes. (Romans 3:10–18)

Before salvation, life in this world is like living in prison, awaiting execution for a capital crime, for "the wages of sin is death" (Romans 3:23). Consequently, for the unrepentant God's sentence is eternal separation from all goodness in a place called hell. Jesus Christ often spoke about the reality of hell and described it as a place of eternal conscious torment where, Jesus said, "the worm does not die, and the fire is not quenched" (Mark 9:42–49).

The book of Revelation tells us that hell will be cast into the lake of fire where the wicked dead will suffer torment forever.

> And the devil that deceived them was cast into the lake of fire and brimstone, where the beast and the false prophet are, and shall be tormented day and night forever and ever ... And whosoever was not found written in the book of life was cast into the lake of fire ... But the fearful, and unbelieving, and the abominable, and murderers, and whoremongers, and sorcerers, and idolaters, and all liars, shall have their part in the lake which burneth with fire and brimstone: which is the second death." (Revelation 20:10, 15; 21:8)

The lake of fire is the destiny for all those who reject God's forgiveness and salvation through Jesus Christ.

And so the Holy Spirit's ministry of conviction

would have us becoming aware that we all deserve an eternity in hell as the just punishment for our sins. Consequently, a person under conviction will experience the fear of the Lord—the recognition that God has the absolute right to judge our eternal fate. For this reason, Jesus Christ warned us to be afraid of God's power to cast people into hell.

> And I say unto you my friends, Be not afraid of them that kill the body, and after that have no more that they can do. But I will forewarn you whom ye shall fear: Fear Him, which after He hath killed hath power to cast into hell; yea, I say unto you, fear Him. (Luke 12:4–5)

But do not misunderstand: the fear of the Lord is a good thing, because the fear of God leads us to faith in God's merciful redemption. As King Solomon said in Proverbs, "The fear of the Lord is a fountain of life, to depart from the snares of death" (Proverbs 14:27). Fearing hell motivates us to seek refuge in God's abundant mercy.

In my Bible study classes, I often ask the question, "What do you deserve from God?" And many will reply, "I deserve respect from God," or "I deserve love from God," or "I deserve health, wealth, and blessing from God." They are genuinely shocked when they discover what the Bible says they deserve: according to scripture, the only thing sinners deserve from God is hell, death, and the grave. Remember, God makes it clear in the book of Romans that "the wages of sin is death" (Romans 6:23).

Spiritual conviction is a gift from God, for it motivates us to seek God's complete forgiveness and deliverance. The gospel message is not about God making our lives satisfied and comfortable. The authentic gospel proclaims the Savior's rescue mission to deliver us from the eternal fate we deserve. And so the question we must all ask ourselves is, "Do you want God's ultimate justice or mercy?" Receiving God's justice means eternal damnation, but receiving God's mercy means forgiveness and everlasting life.

Chapter 9

Anchored by a Broken Heart

*Our heart must be broken, and we ourselves must
be stripped before the healing balm can be applied
and the robe of righteousness can be put upon us.*
Charles Spurgeon,
"Hope for the Worst Backsliders" (1896)

When a prisoner is up for parole, the parole board
wants to determine whether the felon has genuine
remorse for their crimes. As I stated before, life on
earth is like being in prison waiting for execution. God
sets free only those people who have genuine shame
over their sin and rebellion. Appropriate shame is an
attitude that leads to redemption, and hence remorse
over sin is proof of sincere Holy Spirit conviction, for
genuine conviction will break our hearts so that we
mourn over our sin.

Shame's crushing nature brings the kind of humility
required to receive deliverance and forgiveness of sin.

As the psalmist said, "Fill their faces with shame, that they may seek Your name, O Lord" (Psalm 83:16). Without brokenhearted contrition, salvation is impossible.

And so Jesus Christ came as Messiah to heal the brokenhearted, equating iniquity with something that imprisons, oppresses, and breaks the heart.

> The Spirit of the Lord is upon Me, because He hath anointed Me to preach the gospel to the poor; He hath sent me to *heal the brokenhearted,* to preach deliverance to the captives, and recovering of sight to the blind, to set at liberty them that are bruised, to preach the acceptable year of the Lord. (Luke 4:18–19, emphasis added)

Jesus Christ used the term translated into English as "brokenhearted" based on the Old Testament word *daka,* meaning contrite, crushed, beaten in pieces, broken, and humbled, for which the English equivalent is *contrite. Webster's New College Dictionary* defines *contrite* as "to crush, to grind: Repentant for one's sins or inadequacies: Penitent" and *contrition* as "a sincere remorse for wrongdoing." And so a heart grieving over one's sins is the fruit or outworking of genuine repentance. Therefore, contrition is deep mourning and sorrow for violating God's law.

Fortunately, God looks favorably upon brokenhearted contrite sinners before their salvation, as we can see in the following passages.

> The LORD is nigh unto them that are of a broken heart; and saveth such as be of a contrite spirit. (Psalm 34:18)

> The sacrifices of God are a broken spirit: a broken and a contrite heart, O God, thou wilt not despise. (Psalm 51:17)

> For thus saith the high and lofty One that inhabiteth eternity, whose name is Holy; I dwell in the high and holy place, with him also that is of a contrite and humble spirit, to revive the spirit of the humble, and to revive the heart of the contrite ones. (Isaiah 57:15)

> Thus, saith the LORD, "The heaven is My throne, and the earth is My footstool: where is the house that ye build unto Me? And where is the place of my rest? For all those things hath Mine hand made, and all those things have been, saith the LORD: but to this man will I look, even to him that is poor and of a contrite spirit, and trembleth at my word. (Isaiah 66:1–2)

Therefore, Jesus Christ was proclaiming Old Testament scripture when He said,

> Blessed are the poor in spirit: for theirs is the kingdom of heaven. Blessed are they that mourn for they shall be comforted. (Matthew 5:3–4)

Poverty of spirit is recognizing one's total impotence to save oneself. Think of a beggar lying in a gutter, unable to move. This person is so humbled, broken, and needy that his daily survival is entirely dependent on others' charity, and therefore this poor wretch mourns his helpless condition.

Authentic repentance is the painful acknowledgment that personal sin has completely crippled our ability to fix or save ourselves. Before salvation, we are spiritually "dead in trespasses and sins" (Ephesians 2:1), and thus an unforgiven sinner is like a corpse that has lost all its ability to change its condition. By contrast, the contrite recognize their spiritual bankruptcy and give up trying to get eternal life based on good deeds.

Regardless of life's circumstances, God sees the total bankruptcy of each person's spiritual condition before salvation. Consequently, the risen Savior confronted the unredeemed who were members of the Laodicea church. Even though they inhabited a congregation, they were not saved, as evidenced by their lukewarm devotion to Christ. Thus Jesus Christ said to them,

> I know thy works, that thou art neither cold nor hot: I would thou wert cold or hot. So then because thou art lukewarm, and neither cold nor hot, I will spue thee out of my mouth. Because thou sayest, I am rich, and increased with goods, and have need of nothing; and knowest not that thou art wretched, and miserable, and poor, and blind, and naked: I counsel thee to buy of me gold tried in the fire [of contrition], that thou mayest be rich; and white raiment, that thou mayest be clothed, and that the shame of thy nakedness do not appear; and anoint thine eyes with eye salve, that thou mayest see. As many as I love, I rebuke and chasten. Be zealous therefore, and repent. (Revelation 3:15–19)

The Lord equated the pain of fire with the emotional distress of contrition, for true salvation is found in the gold of authentic remorse and humility.

Likewise, the apostle James addressed a group of illegitimate Christians because they did not bear the fruit of genuine salvation. They showed no evidence of contrition or devotion to Christian service, and hence James diagnosed their spiritual condition as unsaved. Therefore, under the Holy Spirit's direction, James recommended they start over by finding authentic brokenhearted repentance. As he said to them,

> Ye adulterers and adulteresses, know ye not that the friendship of the world is enmity with God? Whosoever therefore will be a friend of the world is the enemy of God. Do ye think that the scripture saith in vain, The spirit that dwelleth in us lusteth to envy? But He giveth more grace. Wherefore He saith, God resisteth the proud, but giveth grace unto the humble. Submit yourselves therefore to God. Resist the devil, and he will flee from you. Draw nigh to God, and He will draw nigh to you. Cleanse your hands, ye sinners, and purify your hearts, ye double minded. *Be afflicted, and mourn, and weep: let your laughter be turned to mourning, and* your *joy to heaviness. Humble yourselves in the sight of the Lord, and He shall lift you up.*" (James 4:4–10, emphasis added)

And so the way we draw close to God is always through humility. Moreover, it is imperative to discuss the difference between religion based on false works and proper redemption found only in Jesus Christ. Religious activity is like trying to restore a house beyond repair, and a little work here and minor improvements there will not solve the problem of a condemned foundation. But all false religion promises to make you a better person through their religious system, and by your efforts to make yourself worthy of God. All false religion promotes enhanced spirituality through good deeds, sacred works, ceremonial rites, rituals, sacraments, and priestly interventions. Furthermore, false spirituality teaches that man can solve his disconnect with God, but biblically this premise is in error. The Word of God makes it clear that man cannot make things right with God, and because we are incapable, God therefore must do the work of saving a soul.

Jesus Christ thoroughly condemned the self-righteous who believed they had made themselves worthy of God.

> Ye are they which justify yourselves before men; but God knoweth your hearts: for that which is highly esteemed among men is [an] abomination in the sight of God. (Luke 16:15)

Charles Spurgeon echoed this biblical truth when he said,

> We have not any one of us a righteousness that will stand the test of the all-searching eye of God, and in our heart of hearts we know it is so.[5]

Do not be deceived. No religious organization or so-called holy man has the power to save you. No ritual or sacrament can bring permanent remission of sin. There are not enough prayer beads in the world to repair your corrupt spiritual nature. There are not enough candles or statues to pray to that can fix the foundation of your soul. Only by deep mourning over your spiritual bankruptcy can you prepare to meet the genuine Jesus Christ. And so, if someone is promoting emotionally painless salvation, they are assuredly a false teacher.

God wants you to know the pain of your helpless spiritual condition so that you will place all your faith and hope of salvation in Christ, for the temporary discomfort of contrition will put in you a hunger to be forgiven by God. Old-time preachers understood that we must be made miserable before we can find Christian joy, for the pain of conviction is but a brief time prior to salvation, while the pain of eternal

---

[5] Charles Spurgeon, "Hope for the Worst of Backsliders" (1896).

damnation will never end. Therefore, let God have His way. Surrender to the loving truth that will convict you of the overwhelming weight of your sin. Cry out from the depths of your soul with genuine remorse, and then ask God for His unmerited salvation.

Chapter 10

Anchored by Grace

*They who truly come to God for mercy,
come as beggars, and not as creditors:
they come for mere mercy, for sovereign
grace, and not for anything that is due.*
Jonathan Edwards
"The Works of Jonathan Edwards" (ed. 1852)

Those who are brokenhearted over their sin will want to know that God offers them grace. For grace means getting blessings from God that you do not deserve. Grace means receiving unmerited favor from God, and thus for grace to be grace, it cannot be based on any human merit. The contrite sinner must come to Jesus Christ by faith alone to be saved. The good news is that God offers unworthy sinners salvation based solely on the merit of Christ's righteous life, atoning death, and resurrection from the dead. Hence God offers resurrection life only to those who consider themselves unworthy, for no one deserves God's grace. As the Scriptures confirm, "all have sinned, and come short of the glory of God" (Romans 3:23), but salvation by unmerited favor is offered to every member of the human race.

The apostle Peter had a vision and in the house of Cornelius proclaimed what he discovered.

> And he said unto them, Ye know how that it is an unlawful thing for a man that is a Jew to keep company or come unto one of another nation; but God hath shewed me that I should not call any man common or unclean. (Acts 10:28)

Peter understood that non-Jews could also be saved by faith in Jesus Christ. Through Jesus Christ, God opened the door of salvation to everyone. And so we are reminded that grace means God blesses people of faith with eternal life, even though they are not holy or righteous according to Mosaic law. Salvation is based solely on what Jesus Christ has done to save sinners.

A great example of God's grace to the unworthy is in the Gospel of Matthew. Matthew writes about Jesus Christ's encounter with a Gentile woman who wanted Jesus to deliver her daughter from demonic possession. Based on Mosaic law, this Gentile woman should have been excluded from God's blessing, for

Gentiles were considered unclean. And yet by grace and through faith, she received deliverance for her daughter. As Matthew explains,

> Then Jesus went thence and departed into the coasts of Tyre and Sidon. And behold, a woman of Canaan came out of the same coasts, and cried unto Him, saying, Have mercy on me, O Lord, thou Son of David; my daughter is grievously vexed with a devil. But He answered her not a word. And His disciples came and besought him, saying, Send her away; for she crieth after us. But He answered and said, I am not sent but unto the lost sheep of the house of Israel. Then came she and worshipped Him, saying, Lord, help me. But He answered and said, It is not meet to take the children's bread and to cast it to dogs. And she said, Truth, Lord: yet the dogs eat of the crumbs which fall from their masters' table. Then Jesus answered and said unto her, O woman, great is thy faith, be it unto thee even as thou wilt. And her daughter was made whole from that very hour. (Matthew 15:21–28)

This narrative is a beautiful picture of every person who receives salvation by grace through faith in Jesus Christ. First, like her, they must admit their unworthiness to be saved. Second, they must recognize that Jesus Christ is the true Messiah, the Son of David. And like her, they must persist in faith, believing in the Lord's goodness to deliver them despite their unworthiness. For everyone must trust Christ's goodness and grace to be saved.

Before salvation, our sins make us spiritually dead to God. The unsaved are entirely unable to change their spiritual condition. Only by God's power and unmerited favor can our lost state be changed, and only by God's grace can an unworthy sinner be made spiritually alive. For God's Word says,

> But God, who is rich in mercy, for His great love wherewith He loved us, *even when we were dead in sins, hath quickened us together with Christ, (by grace ye are saved;)* And hath raised us up together, and made us sit together in heavenly places in Christ Jesus: That in the ages to come He might shew the exceeding riches of His grace in His kindness toward us through Christ Jesus. *For by grace are ye saved through faith; and that not of yourselves: it is the gift of*

God: Not of works, lest any man should boast. (Ephesians 2:4–9, emphasis added)

In the narrative of the Gentile woman, we see Christ casting out a demon that had possessed the woman's daughter. And thus, we notice, Jesus confirms the reality of evil spiritual beings called demons. Initially, spirit beings were created by God to serve and glorify Him. They were given free will to love and serve God or rebel and serve themselves. But one of these angels, named Lucifer, decided to exalt and serve himself instead of God, consequently falling into sin and error. As the prophet Isaiah writes,

How art thou fallen from heaven, O Lucifer, son of the morning! how art thou cut down to the ground, which didst weaken the nations! For thou hast said in thine heart, I will ascend into heaven. I will exalt my throne above the stars of God: I will sit also upon the mount of the congregation, in the sides of the north: I will ascend above the heights of the clouds; I will be like the Highest. Yet thou shalt be brought down to hell, to the sides of the pit. (Isaiah 14:12–15)

Because Lucifer rebelled, God changed his name to Satan, meaning one who opposes God. Satan and a third of the angels rebelled against the Lord, and because of their rebellion, the nature of these spirit beings changed from good to evil. They became demons that exist to oppose and resist the gospel of grace. And so Satan is the spiritual father of those who resist the ministry of Jesus Christ and the gospel of salvation by grace. For Jesus said,

> If God were your Father, ye would love Me: for I proceeded forth and came from God; neither came I of Myself, but He sent me. Why do ye not understand My speech? Even because ye cannot hear My word. Ye are of your father the devil, and the lusts of your father ye will do. He was a murderer from the beginning, and abode not in the truth, because there is no truth in him. When he speaketh a lie, he speaketh of his own: for he is a liar, and the father of it. And because I tell you the truth, ye believe Me not. Which of you convicteth Me of sin? And if I say the truth, why do ye not believe Me? He that is of God heareth God's words: ye therefore hear them not, because ye are not of God. (John 8:42–47)

The apostle Paul likewise informs us that all unbelievers are in league with Satan.

> And you hath He quickened, who were dead in trespasses and sins; Wherein in time past ye walked according to the course of this world, according to the prince of the power of the air, [Satan] the spirit that now worketh in the children of disobedience: Among whom also we all had our conversation in times past in the lusts of our flesh, fulfilling the desires of the flesh and of the mind; and were by nature the children of wrath, even as others. (Ephesians 2:1–3)

Subsequently, Satan has invented every false anti-grace religion as the ultimate opposer of God's will. These false religions reject the concept of God's unmerited favor and instead promote deceptive doctrines of salvation based on personal self-effort and religious activity. Therefore, Satan either wants you to believe the lie that your sins exclude you from redemption, or he wants you to think that you can make yourself worthy of God. Either way, Satan gets people to abandon faith in God's grace. And without grace, they are doomed to hell.

Therefore, people reject God's grace because

they fall prey to false demonic teachings. But God commands us to abstain from all fraudulent religious activity and instructions, as defined in Deuteronomy 18, as all wrong spiritual practices can lead to demonic oppression or possession.

> When thou art come into the land which the LORD thy God giveth thee, thou shalt not learn to do after the abominations of those nations. There shall not be found among you anyone that maketh his son or his daughter to pass through the fire, [child sacrifice] or that divination, or an observer of times, [astrology] or an enchanter, or a witch, Or a charmer, or a consulter with familiar spirits, or a wizard, or a necromancer. For all that do these things are an abomination unto the LORD: and because of these abominations the LORD thy God doth drive them out from before thee. Thou shalt be perfect with the LORD thy God. For these nations, which thou shalt possess, hearkened unto observers of times, and unto diviners: but as for thee, the LORD thy God hath not suffered thee so to do. (Deuteronomy 18:9–12a)

People can ultimately be possessed by demons when they rebel against God's warnings and practice the occult. Hence, the demon-possessed are most unworthy to receive deliverance and salvation, for they have openly rebelled against the protective statutes of God. And yet, even these people by God's unmerited favor can be saved by Jesus Christ. Every time Jesus cast out a demon, He demonstrated His divine love and grace to the unworthy. Because all spiritual deliverance and salvation come by God's unmerited favor, the apostle Paul writes of Christ

> Who hath delivered us from the power of darkness, and hath translated us into the kingdom of His dear Son: In whom we have redemption through his blood, even the forgiveness of sins: He has delivered us from the power of darkness and translated us into the kingdom of the Son of His love, in whom we have redemption through His blood, the forgiveness of sins. (Colossians 1:13–14)

Furthermore, by grace God adopts us into His family. As the apostle John wrote,

> But as many as received Him, to them gave He power to become the sons of

God, even to them that believe on His
name: Which were born, not of blood,
nor of the will of the flesh, nor of the will
of man, but of God. (John 1:12–13)

The apostle Paul declared,

For ye have not received the spirit of
bondage again to fear; *but ye have
received the Spirit of adoption*, whereby
we cry, Abba, Father. The Spirit itself
beareth witness with our spirit, that we
are the children of God: And if children,
then heirs; heirs of God, and joint-heirs
with Christ; if so be that we suffer with
Him, that we may be also glorified
together. (Roman's 8:15–17, emphasis
added)

For this reason, adoption is a glorious picture of
God's grace, because the power and will to adopt
resides solely with the potential parent. Likewise, the
power of spiritual adoption resides exclusively with
the divine favor of God. Picture an orphanage: the
children cannot choose the adoptive father, and even
if they want to be selected or ask to be selected, it
does them no good unless the Father favors them.
Therefore, the Father gives unmerited favor to the

child when He adopts them into his family. Hence faith in the Father's goodness is the only requirement for the child to receive adoption. And thus, through His Son, God the Father has provided everything required for spiritual adoption, based solely on grace. For God intends to adopt everyone who comes to Him by faith.

Furthermore, by grace God pardons the wayward sinner. I will discuss the pardon of God again in a later chapter, but it is important to remember that God pardons sinners by His unmerited favor. For the Lord said,

> And I will cleanse them from all their iniquity, whereby they have sinned against Me; and *I will pardon all their iniquities*, whereby they have sinned, and whereby they have transgressed against Me. (Jeremiah 33:8, emphasis added)

And finally, by grace, a great blessing is given called imputed righteousness. The word "imputed" means something deposited into an account. Thus all the sins of the unsaved are accounted against them by God. At the great white throne judgment, accounting books are opened, and all the evil deeds and sins we have committed are registered.

And I saw a great white throne, and Him that sat on it, from whose face the earth and the heaven fled away; and there was found no place for them. And I saw the dead, small, and great, stand before God; and the books were opened: and another book was opened, which is the book of life: and the dead were judged out of those things which were written in the books, according to their works. And the sea gave up the dead which were in it; and death and hell delivered up the dead which were in them: and they were judged every man according to their works. And death and hell were cast into the lake of fire. This is the second death. And whosoever was not found written in the book of life was cast into the lake of fire. (Revelation 20:11–15)

Thus every sin is an eternal debt applied to your account, but the grace of God is the solution that removes this mountain of spiritual debt.

The apostle Paul wrote,

What shall we say then that Abraham our father, as pertaining to the flesh, hath found? For if Abraham were justified by works, he hath whereof to glory, but notbefore God. For what saith the Scripture? *Abraham believed God, and it was counted unto him for righteousness.* Now to him that worketh is the reward not reckoned of grace, but of debt. *But to him that worketh not, but believeth on Him that justifieth the ungodly, his faith is counted for righteousness.* (Romans 4:1–5. emphasis added)

When you place all your sins at the foot of the cross, trusting in God's grace, then the Lord will remove your debt and impute into your spiritual account the very righteousness of Jesus Christ. And thus, by grace, we are made righteous.

Captain John Newton (1725–1807) was an evil man who operated a slave ship. One night in a violent storm at sea, God convicted him of his cruel ways. Newton then renounced his sins and in deep remorse sought the Lord, thereby discovering the gospel of grace. He was saved by the unmerited favor of God. Once saved, Newton spent the rest of his life preaching salvation by grace and fighting the slave trade. And it was John Newton who penned these sublime words,

Amazing grace how sweet the sound
that saved a wretch like me!

I once was lost but now am found,
was blind but now I see.[6]

Like John Newton, we too must find God's amazing grace to receive salvation, deliverance, adoption, pardon, and imputed righteousness.

---

[6] John Newton, "Amazing Grace," *Olney Hymns (1779).*

Chapter 11

Anchored through Faith

*Faith receiveth the promise, embraceth it, and
comforteth the soul unspeakably with it. Faith
is so great an artist in arguing and reasoning
with the soul, that it will bring over the hardest
heart that it hath to deal with. It will bring to my
remembrance at once, both my vileness against
God, and His goodness towards me; it will show
me, that though I deserve not to breathe in the
air, yet that God will have me an heir of glory.*
John Bunyan
"The Works of John Bunyan: Experimental,
doctrinal, and practical" (ed.1850)

Grace is the will and power of God that saves us.
But faith is the attitude we need to receive the saving
power of God. For faith is a trusting reliance on the
truth and goodness of God. To illustrate faith, imagine
you have terminal cancer, but the doctor told you that

eight ounces of a blue liquid would entirely heal you. And so, by faith in your doctor, you would quickly swallow that medicine to the last drop.

Grace is like the medicine that must be consumed to save, and faith is the act of swallowing that medicine. For once consumed by faith, the grace of God will do its work to save and transform a soul. But without faith, the saving power of God remains unreceived. For the scripture tells us,

> For by grace are ye saved through faith;
> and that not of yourselves: it is the gift of
> God: Not of works, lest any man should
> boast. (Ephesians 2:8–9)

Personal faith is a belief in God's truth, power, goodness, and His Son, Jesus Christ. It is only by faith in God that we can be redeemed.

To further illustrate faith, picture God's saving work and power as eating a meal at a restaurant. Like a chef, God mixes all the saving ingredients. He provides the sacrifice. He raises Jesus Christ from the dead, and He fulfills all the prophecies and promises concerning salvation. Finally, God places the finished product before you. And because you have faith in the goodness of this divine chef, you sit down to consume this salvation meal.

Authentic faith happens when you act upon your

trust in the chef and eat the meal. For faith is your willingness to apply the saving grace of God to your spiritual system. Faith is not a matter of placing trust in oneself, because we did nothing to prepare this salvation.

Just as eating does not change the quality of the meal, our faith does not alter the quality of God's salvation. The fork does not change the substance of a meal. The quality and perfection of Christ's work to save us are the same whether someone believes it or not.

Consequently, unbelief restrains people from receiving the available saving grace of God, for they refuse to trust and partake in the excellent salvation provided. Salvation is unobtainable to those who refuse to believe. As Jesus Christ said,

> He that believeth on him (Jesus) is not condemned: but he that believeth not is condemned already, because he hath not believed in the name of the only begotten Son of God. (John 3:18)

Salvation is impossible without faith in what God has done to save us. Authentic faith is based on the substance of God's salvation promises.

The essence of Christian faith is biblical evidence. As the writer of the book of Hebrews declares,

> Now faith is the *substance* of things
> hoped for, the *evidence* of things not
> seen. (Hebrews 11:1 emphasis added)

Hence authentic faith conforms to the evidence found in the Word of God. As William Tyndale proclaimed,

> To have faith, therefore, or a trust in
> anything, where God hath not promised,
> is plain idolatry, and a worshiping of
> thine own imagination instead of God.[7]

Thus only in the Bible can we find the authentic information needed to build our faith.

Unfortunately, some people think faith is a power source unto itself. They believe they have the power to create their spiritual reality, and so they feel that just because they believe something, it must be true. They have bought into the lie that faith is a cosmic force with inherent power. But true faith is always a belief in God's reality as defined by His Word.

Reality does not change based on the whims and beliefs of man. You must ask yourself a series of questions. Does the nature of God change because you exist? Can the truth of God vary based on what you believe? Does the reality of sin and redemption

---

[7] William Tindale, (1494-1536) The Obedience of a Christian Man & How Christian Rulers Out to Govern

change because of your philosophy? Of course not. For the truth is always consistent with God, no matter your propensities, existence, or false beliefs.

Saving faith must agree with God's revelation about deliverance from sin and damnation. True faith can only be a belief in the salvation that God prepared. For this reason, true faith is like eating at Mom's house. In Mom's home, only one meal is served each evening. And so, by faith, you must die to your desires and humbly receive the meal Mom serves. So too does true faith deny self and surrender to God's plan for salvation. Beyond salvation, faith is daily surrendering to God's will.

One of the most significant Biblical illustrations of learning to live by faith is found in Jacob's history. The book of Genesis tells us that one day Esau, Jacob's older brother, was extremely hungry. Jacob used this situation to manipulate Esau into selling away his birthright to Jacob. Because Jacob's father Isaac was blind, Jacob tricked him into giving Esau's blessing to him, for Jacob was living up to his name, which means "one who usurps." Even though Jacob believed in and wanted God's benefits, Jacob lacked faith in God's way of providing these blessings. Jacob rationalized getting what he wanted through manipulation and deceit instead of trusting God's will.

Jacob had to learn to trust God the hard way through sowing and reaping, because the Bible tells us that sowing our lives in disobedience will bring destruction. But trusting in God brings goodness, peace, and eternal life. As the apostle Paul wrote,

> Be not deceived; God is not mocked: for whatsoever a man soweth, that shall he also reap. For he that soweth to his flesh shall of the flesh reap corruption; but he that soweth to the Spirit shall of the Spirit reap life everlasting. (Galatians 6:7–8)

And because Jacob sowed seeds of deception, Esau sought to kill him, forcing Jacob to abandon his material possessions and family to flee for his life. Consequently, Jacob was forced into a long journey to find his mother's brother, Laban.

Jacob placed his faith in his ability to trick and manipulate people instead of in God. God would then use Jacob's circumstances to teach him how to trust God's way. As God's providence would have it, Jacob's trickery led him to live as a servant to his Uncle Laban. And as it turned out, Uncle Laban was more manipulative and cunning than Jacob.

At first, Jacob agreed to work for Laban for seven years to acquire his beautiful daughter Rachel as his bride. But seven years later, Laban tricked Jacob into lying with his plain daughter Leah on their wedding night. So Leah, not Rachel, was Jacob's wife. Jacob then agreed to another seven-year term of service to make Rachel his second wife. Thus, by the time he married Rachel, Jacob had worked for his uncle for fourteen years. But Jacob had nothing but his wives and growing family to show for it.

Then Jacob, still not functioning in faith, decided to trick his father-in-law. Jacob agreed to work for Laban for another seven years if all the inferior speckled sheep born during that time became his property because Jacob had figured out a tricky way to get Laban's superior sheep to breed with his inferior ones. As a result, a significant number of the herd became speckled sheep and Jacob's property.

Because of the trickery, Laban began to resent Jacob. So after twenty-one years of service, Jacob thought it best to leave Laban and head home to Canaan. Jacob snuck away by night with his wives, concubines, children, servants, and herds, making Laban furious. With a small army of servants, Laban chased after Jacob. Fortunately, once caught, Jacob was able to work out a deal with Laban to separate and avoid trouble. But part of that deal was Jacob could never return to the territory of Laban.

Still Jacob's troubles were far from over, for upon his return to the promised land, Jacob had to deal with his brother Esau. Jacob would have to encounter the man who, twenty-one years earlier, had sworn to kill him the next time they met. Jacob was trapped by the consequences of his bad behavior: he could not go back, and he dreaded going forward.

Eventually, Jacob's caravan approached the territory of Esau. It was reported that Esau was on his way with an army to intercept his hated brother. In desperation to save himself, Jacob started to give away all he had to Esau, hoping to appease his brother's wrath. First, he sent his flocks and herds. Then Jacob sent his servants. Jacob even gave away his wives and children to be the slaves of Esau. Finally, there was nothing left to give, and Jacob was left alone in the night.

Allowing dire circumstances is often God's plan when He seeks to redeem a soul. Like Jacob, to save us the Lord often allows life to take away what we love and desire. And sometimes, what we sow in life will leave us with nothing but the promise of personal salvation. For Jesus Christ proclaimed,

> He that findeth his life shall lose it: and he that loseth his life for My sake shall find it." (Matthew 10:39)

And likewise,

> For whosoever will save his life shall lose it; but whosoever shall lose his life for My sake and the gospel's, the same shall

save it. For what shall it profit a man, if he shall gain the whole world, and lose his own soul? Or what shall a man give in exchange for his soul? (Mark 8:35–37)

Furthermore, Jesus told us

The kingdom of heaven is like unto a merchant man, seeking goodly pearls: Who, when he had found one pearl of great price, went and sold all that he had, and bought it. (Matthew 13:45–46)

Jesus Christ wants us to know that salvation is the one essential thing we must have. Jesus Christ is that pearl of great price which gives eternal life. Eternal salvation is worth all you are, all you have, and all you will be. For Jesus Christ can save even when the follies of life have left us nothing. The ultimate gift of eternal life has nothing to do with temporary health and prosperity. When you die, you will lose everything you have. As Job said,

Naked came I out of my mother's womb, and naked shall I return thither: the LORD gave, and the LORD hath taken away; blessed be the name of the LORD. (Job 1:21)

But Jesus offers eternal life to those who have lost everything the world has to offer. Jesus can provide eternal life to people who suffer from terminal illnesses and give abundant spiritual life to the crippled and infirmed, because eternal life transcends material reality. As the apostle Paul said, Christ "hath delivered us from the power of darkness, and hath translated us into the kingdom of his dear Son" (Colossians 1:13).

Let us return to Jacob's story. The Bible tells us that he was alone in the dark when he met the Angel of the Lord. And this angel we recognize as the pre-incarnate Jesus Christ. But Jacob was afraid and wrestled against Him; hence Jacob's struggle with God symbolizes our faith struggle. In our fallen nature, we do not want to surrender our will to God. And so God, by His unwavering love, wrestles against our foolish desires and prideful hearts by allowing circumstances to challenge our thinking.

As daylight approached, the Angel of the Lord touched the hip socket of Jacob, crippling him, and then started to move away. But suddenly, Jacob realized his pride and folly, and instead of fighting the will of the Lord, by faith he clung to Christ instead. Jacob held onto the Lord and refused to let go, for Jacob's faith was no longer focused on material blessings but rather on being personally connected to God. Thus, with enduring faith, Jacob became anchored to the God who saves.

Jesus Christ also requires us to have enduring faith for salvation, saying, "he who endures to the end shall be saved" (Matthew 24:13). In the book of Hebrews, there is a mention of great faith heroes who did not receive material blessings in this life. But these great servants of God had enduring faith that looked past materialism and onward to heavenly life and the resurrection to come.

> And others had trial of cruel mockings and scourgings, yea, more-over of bonds and imprisonment: (Of whom the world was not worthy:) they wandered in deserts, and in mountains, and in dens and caves of the earth. And these all, having obtained a good report through faith, received not the promise: God having provided some better thing for us, that they without us should not be made perfect. (Hebrews 11:36–40)

Therefore, when Jacob the usurper lost everything, he tenaciously clung to his Savior by faith. God made Jacob a new man by grace alone, through faith alone. And from that moment on, Jacob would live his life as a chosen vessel for the Lord. For when Jacob found God, he found salvation and his true self. For this reason, God renamed him Israel, meaning "the father of many nations, the servant of the Lord."

Soon afterward, Jacob discovered Esau had forgiven him. And graciously, Esau allowed Jacob to return to the land of his father. Esau even refused all the gifts that Jacob had offered him. And so God restored unto Jacob all that he had, and Jacob had learned to hold on to the Savior by faith when all seemed lost.

Chapter 12

Anchored by the Cross

*May we sit at the foot of the cross; and
there learn what sin has done, what
justice has done, what love has done.*
John Newton
letter to the Reverend William Bull (1847)

*To Him who loved us and washed us
from our sins in His own blood.*
Revelation 1:5

Good Friday is the most critical day in the Christian calendar, for on that day, Jesus Christ conquered our sin by the shedding of His blood. In the Gospel of John (19:30), the last word Jesus spoke on the cross was, in Greek, *Tetelestai,* "It is finished." And this word has the precise meaning of something thoroughly completed, or an act completed in full measure, like a cup filled to the brim, unable to hold even one more drop of water. Thus the gift of Jesus Christ on the cross completely fulfilled the righteous penalty God required for the world's sins, and when Jesus died on the cross, the punishment for our sins was completed.

The famous scripture John 3:16 is often quoted out of context:

> For God so loved the world, that He gave His only begotten Son, that whosoever believeth in Him should not perish, but have everlasting life.

By itself, this passage can be taken to mean you should believe in Him generically to gain everlasting life, or just believe in Him superficially, so you won't perish. But this misses the point.

When I was in college, I attended a friend's wedding reception. I remember having a conversation with the groom about his concept of religion and Christ. He boldly stated that his entire religion was based on John 3:16, adding, "The Bible says that if I believe in Jesus, I will receive eternal life. So, because I believe Jesus existed, and I believe He was a real person, therefore I must have eternal life."

But there is a problem with this kind of oversimplification of scripture. For John 3:16 by itself is not even a complete thought on salvation. Instead, it is one part of a more comprehensive statement spoken by the Lord. The proper understanding of the word "believe" is based on the passage's whole context, for Jesus is not telling us to believe in his historical existence to be redeemed—He is saying we must believe certain things about Him to receive everlasting life.

So let us look at the third chapter of John in its greater context. Christ was speaking to Nicodemus about the necessity of being spiritually born again to be saved. And because Nicodemus did not understand, Jesus continued to expound on what must be believed to obtain this new birth.

> Art thou a master of Israel, and knowest not these things? Verily, verily, I say unto thee, We speak that we do know, and testify that we have seen; and ye receive not our witness. If I have told you earthly things, and ye believe not, how shall ye believe, if I tell you of heavenly things? And no man hath ascended up to heaven, but He that came down from heaven, even the Son of man which is in heaven. *And as Moses lifted up the serpent in the wilderness, even so must the Son of man be lifted up: That whosoever believeth in Him should not perish but have eternal life.* For God so loved the world, that

He gave his only begotten Son, that whosoever believeth in Him should not perish, but have everlasting life. (John 3:10–16 emphasis added)

So what did Jesus require of Nicodemus to believe? First, he was expected to believe the Son of Man was directly sent from heaven. Second, Nicodemus must accept Jesus Christ as the Son of Man, the Messiah. And third, and perhaps most puzzling, Nicodemus had to believe that Jesus, the Son of Man, must be lifted like the bronze serpent in the day of Moses.

Now, the bronze serpent of Moses had deep prophetic meaning about the purpose of the coming Messiah. In the book of Numbers, chapter 21, God brought judgment against the nation of Israel for their rebellion in the wilderness. Consequently, God sent poisonous snakes to bite the children of Israel, and they became sick unto death. Because they were ill and dying, the people cried out to God with contrition and repentance.

Therefore, God commanded Moses to make a bronze serpent mounted on a wooden pole and then to lift the serpent for all the people to see, for in scripture a snake symbolizes Satan and sin. When the people looked upon the bronze serpent, a symbol of sin crucified, they were healed because of God's mercy.

So what Jesus was telling Nicodemus is that the

Son of Man's death would be like lifting the bronze serpent, and thus sin was to be crucified on the cross. Christ Himself would die to destroy the power of sin. As people look with faith at Jesus crucified, they too will be healed with eternal life. Therefore, only by believing in Christ's atoning death can we receive new life. As Augustine noted in his exegesis on the Gospel of John, (*the Tractatus*), "The Jews looked upon a serpent to be freed from serpents, and we look upon the death of Christ to be delivered from death."

Moreover, the bronze serpent is symbolic of the sacrificial system of the Jews. For animal sacrifice was thoroughly embedded within the Jewish mindset at the time of Jesus. Since the beginning of man, the purpose of animal sacrifice has been to cover sin and shame to make oneself right with God. God slew the first animal to cover the shame and nakedness of Adam and Eve after their fall, and thus this sacrifice was God's first act of mercy toward sinful humanity. After God delivered Moses and the children of Israel from the oppression of Pharaoh, He instituted the Hebrew sacrificial system. In so doing, God ordained that "almost all things are by the law purged with blood; and without shedding of blood is no remission" (Hebrews 9:22).

Therefore, each time someone sinned in Israel, they were required by law to sacrifice an animal at the temple as a sin offering, for this offering would temporarily cover their sin. Moreover, in the Old Testament the ultimate sin offering was the blood of a lamb. So before God delivered Israel out of Egypt, God brought judgment upon the Egyptians for their idolatry and cruel bondage of God's chosen people. Consequently, God put ten plagues upon the Egyptians, the final of which was death to all the firstborn in the land of Egypt. However, because God is merciful, He provided a way to avoid the firstborn child's death. Each family was to sacrifice a lamb and place its blood on the doorpost of their house. Every home marked by blood would be spared the firstborn's death. Because of this blood atonement, death passed over.

The Hebrew word for atonement is *kaphar,* which means to cover something. Therefore, the act of atonement is a covering of sin. Blood atonement is an act that cancels sin and appeases God so that He will forgive, pardon, and purge away sin. Atonement requires a blood sacrifice that reconciles the guilty sinner to God. The atoning sacrifice transfers the guilt of the sin to the innocent animal. As Charles Spurgeon stated,

> Throughout the Old Testament this was always the idea of a sin-offering—that of a perfect victim; without offense on its own account, taking the place of the offender; the transference of the

offender's sin to that victim, and that expiation in the person of the victim for the sins done by another.[8]

Ever since the first Passover, lamb's blood has been the symbol of an atonement that restores God's mercy to His children. God commanded the Israelites to celebrate Passover every year to remind them of His great deliverance. And within this context, the words of John the Baptist take on special meaning. For John said of Jesus Christ,

Behold the Lamb of God, which taketh away the sin of the world. (John 1:29)

However, we often romanticize temple worship and the sacrificial system of the Jews. The temple was a grand building dedicated to prayer and worship, but we must also realize that it was a giant slaughterhouse where the blood of sheep, bulls, goats, and birds ran continuously—a place where animal entrails were burnt daily on the brazen altar. Even with the most sophisticated sanitary systems, it is hard to eliminate a slaughterhouse's stench or remove the pungent odor of burning entrails. The harsh smell of the Temple of Jerusalem was God's way of illustrating the corrupt nature of our sin. The sacrificial system was a daily

---

[8] Charles Spurgeon, Expiantion, Sermon 561, Isa. 53:10

object lesson about God's holiness compared to man's gross sinfulness. The sacrificial system demonstrated our need for a permanent atonement.

In our modern world, we are disconnected from the reality of death, for we see meat wrapped in the grocery store instead of having to kill the animals ourselves. And the dead are embalmed to look like china dolls instead of us having to see the twisted reality of rigor mortis. But those living in the time of Christ were intimately aware of the cruelty of death upon their loved ones. Besides, by design, you would pick out a spotless lamb from your sheepfold each year. And for a season, you and your children would pamper that lamb so it would be accepted as a temple sacrifice. Sometimes, the lamb would be like a favorite pet that everyone in the family adored. But during Passover, you would kill this lamb as a sacrifice for your sins in obedience to God. Finally, you would eat this lamb to remember God's power to save you from death. The sacrifice of your lamb and your many other sin offerings each year would continuously remind you of your sinfulness. Therefore, the purpose of the temple system was to continually break your heart about falling short of God's righteous standard. For the Lord said,

> The sacrifices of God are a broken spirit:
> a broken and a contrite heart, O God,
> thou wilt not despise. (Psalm 51:17)

The sacrificial system was a daily reminder of God's hatred of sin and the cost associated with iniquity. Blood sacrifice was instituted as a symbol that prepared people for the permanent solution found only in the sacrifice of Jesus Christ on the cross. As the writer of the book of Hebrews said,

> For it is not possible that the blood of bulls and of goats should take away sins. Wherefore when He cometh into the world, He saith, Sacrifice and offering thou wouldest not, but a body hast thou prepared me: In burnt offerings and sacrifices for sin Thou hast had no pleasure. Then said I, 'Lo, I come (in the volume of the book it is written of me,) to do Thy will, O God.' Above when He said, 'Sacrifice and offering and burnt offerings and offering for sin thou wouldest not, neither hadst pleasure therein; which are offered by the law; Then said He, Lo, I come to do thy will, O God.' He taketh away the first [sacrificial system], that He may establish the second. By the

which will *we are sanctified through the offering of the body of Jesus Christ once for all.* And every priest standeth daily ministering and offering oftentimes the same sacrifices, which can never take away sins: But this man, after He had offered one sacrifice for sins forever, sat down on the right hand of God; From henceforth expecting till His enemies be made his footstool. *For by one offering He hath perfected forever them that are sanctified.'* (Hebrews 10:4–14, emphasis added)

The Son of God's primary purpose was to die for the world's sins, for Jesus Christ left His throne in heaven to become the man who would deliberately lay down his life as the one ultimate and final blood sacrifice. Because Jesus was fully a man, He could be the substitute for all the sins of humanity. And because Jesus was also fully God, He could bear the eternal weight and punishment for all sin. As the apostle Paul said,

And, having made peace through the blood of His cross, by Him to reconcile all things unto Himself; by Him, I say, whether they be things in Earth or things in Heaven. And you, that were sometime alienated and enemies in your mind by wicked works, yet now hath He reconciled in the body of his flesh through death, to present you holy and unblameable and unreproveable in his sight: If ye continue in the faith grounded and settled, and be not moved away from the hope of the gospel, which ye have heard, and which was preached to every creature which is under heaven; whereof I Paul am made a minister. (Colossians 1:20–23)

Our Lord came to bear the eternal righteous penalty that all people deserve from a holy and just God. God the Father transferred all guilt and sin to God the Son. Hence God Himself paid the righteous penalty for our sin, for He took our place on the cross. Therefore, eternal death passes over all who put their faith in the shed blood of Jesus Christ, for He is the Eternal Lamb of God. Salvation comes by faith when we metaphorically place the blood of the lamb on the doorpost of our hearts. As the apostle Peter wrote,

For as much as ye know that ye were not redeemed with corruptible things, as silver and gold, from your vain conversation received by tradition from your fathers,

> *But with the precious blood of Christ, as*
> *of a lamb without blemish and without*
> *spot.* (1 Peter 1:18–19, emphasis added)

Moreover, the cross has a meaning broader than atonement. The cross also means an act of propitiation, which turns the wrath of God away from one person and onto the object of sacrifice. Thus Jesus Christ not only covers our sins by atonement but also turns the wrath of God onto Himself and away from us. Consequently, God's righteous wrath is removed from all who believe in the power of the cross. For as Paul said in the book of Romans,

> For all have sinned and come short of the glory of God; Being justified freely by his grace through the redemption that is in Christ Jesus: Whom God hath set forth to be a *propitiation* through faith in His blood, to declare His righteousness for the remission of sins that are past, through the forbearance of God; To declare, I say, at this time His righteousness: that He might be just, and the justifier of him which believeth in Jesus. (Romans 3:23–26, emphasis added)

For this reason, Jesus Christ volunteered to experience the wrath of God so believers in His atoning death could receive eternal life.

Finally, the cross provides a complete pardon from God through His act of justification. "Pardon" is the concept by which all guilt for a crime is expunged— that is, the former criminal is declared righteous and afforded all the rights of a free citizen. So the moment we place our faith in the atoning death and shed blood of Jesus Christ, God the Father pardons and redeems us, enabling us to serve Him freely. For as the apostle Paul wrote,

> Through the forbearance of God; To declare, I say, at this time His righteousness: *that He might be just, and the justifier of him which believeth in Jesus.* (Romans 3:26, emphasis added)

> For when we were yet without strength, in due time Christ died for the ungodly. For scarcely for a righteous man will one die yet peradventure for a good man some would even dare to die. But God commendeth His love toward us, in that, while we were yet sinners, Christ died for us. Much more then, being now justified by His blood, we shall be saved from

wrath through Him. For if, when we were enemies, *we were reconciled to God by the death of His Son,* much more, being reconciled, we shall be saved by His life. (Romans 5:6–9, emphasis added)

In this way, Christ's atoning sacrifice reconciles us eternally to God the Father. Hence saving faith means understanding that Jesus Christ must become your personal and perpetual sacrifice for sin—that Jesus Christ must become your bronze serpent lifted to heal you spiritually. Jesus wants you to see Him as your individual Passover lamb and your eternal sin offering. That is what Jesus meant when He said,

For verily, verily, I say unto you, except ye eat the flesh of the Son of Man, and drink His blood, ye have no life in you. *Whoso eateth My flesh, and drinketh My blood, hath eternal life; and I will raise him up at the last day.* For My flesh is meat indeed, and My blood is drink indeed. He that eateth My flesh, and drinketh My blood, dwelleth in Me, and I in him. As the living Father hath sent Me, and I live by the Father: so, he that eateth me, even he shall live by me. This is that bread which came down from heaven: not as your fathers did eat manna and are dead: He that eateth of this bread shall live forever. (John 6:53–58 emphasis added)

So by faith, you must devour Christ's death as your very own sacrificial lamb. And you must, by faith, apply that remission of sin directly to your heart and soul. You must believe that the death of Christ was necessary to turn God's righteous wrath away from you. Thus you must see yourself placing the bloody body of the Lord on the altar of your heart. For our sins nailed Jesus to the cross, whipped and beat Him beyond recognition, placed a crown of thorns on His head, pierced His hands and feet, and plunged a spear in His side. Therefore, Jesus Christ commands you to see the cross as your solution for sin.

Finally, Jesus wants you to understand that faith in His shed blood will give you everlasting life. So, take up the blood of Jesus Christ, the Lamb of God, and place it forever on the doorpost of your heart, mind, and soul, so that eternal death can pass over you.

Chapter 13

Anchored by Resurrection Life

*The resurrection of Jesus Christ from the dead
is one of the best attested facts on record. There
were so many witnesses to behold it, that if we
do in the least degree receive the credibility
of men's testimonies, we cannot and we dare
not doubt that Jesus rose from the dead.*
Charles Spurgeon
"The Resurrection of the Dead" (1856)

*For you will not abandon My soul to Sheol
or let your Holy One see corruption.*
Psalm 16:10

The resurrection of Jesus Christ provides hope to
every believer that they too will conquer death. The
goal of a Christian is to receive resurrection life: a
partial impartation of eternal life now called the new

birth, and a complete impartation of eternal life at the resurrection.

The Greek word used in the Bible for the resurrection is *anastasis*, meaning the resuscitation of a corpse to wholeness. The body of Jesus Christ was physically brought back to life and elevated to a perfect, eternal, and glorified state. Without belief in Christ's bodily resurrection, we cannot be saved. The apostle Paul tells us the importance of Christ's resurrection.

> But what saith it? The word is nigh thee, even in thy mouth, and in thy heart: that is, the word of faith, which we preach; That if thou shalt confess with thy mouth the Lord Jesus, and shalt believe in thine heart that God hath raised Him from the dead, thou shalt be saved. (Romans 10:8–9)

However, before we believe in Christ's resurrection, we must first believe Jesus died on the cross. As the apostle John, an eyewitness of Christ's crucifixion and burial, tells us,

> But when they came to Jesus, and saw that He was dead already, they brake not His legs: But one of the soldiers with a spear pierced His side, and forthwith

came there out blood and water. And he that saw it bare record, and his record is true: and he knoweth that he saith true, that ye might believe. For these things were done, that the Scripture should be fulfilled, A bone of Him shall not be broken. And again, another Scripture saith, 'They shall look on Him whom they pierced.' And after this Joseph of Arimathaea, being a disciple of Jesus, but secretly for fear of the Jews, besought Pilate that he might take away the body of Jesus: and Pilate gave him leave. He came therefore and took the body of Jesus. And there also came Nicodemus, which at the first came to Jesus by night, and brought a mixture of myrrh and aloes, about a hundred-pound weight. Then took they the body of Jesus, and wrapped it in linen cloths with the spices, as the manner of the Jews is to bury. Now in the place where He was crucified there was a garden; and in the garden a new sepulchre, wherein was never man yet laid. There laid they Jesus therefore because of the Jews' preparation day; for the sepulchre was nigh at hand. (John 19:33–42)

As John's eyewitness account shows, no one could have survived the scourging, beatings, and crucifixion that Jesus suffered. Roman soldiers were expert executioners, and they confirmed the death of Jesus by stabbing Him in the side with a spear, which caused water and blood to pour from His side.

The lifeless body of Christ was taken down from the cross and wrapped in strips of linen from head to toe. Then the linens were coated with about a hundred pounds of myrrh and aloes. This mummification would have cut off any air supply to Jesus's lungs. Christ lay in this state from Friday afternoon until early Sunday morning. So most assuredly, Jesus was dead in the tomb.

As predicted in the Old Testament, the Messiah was raised to life on the third day. As the apostle Matthew narrates,

> In the end of the sabbath, as it began to dawn toward the first day of the week, came Mary Magdalene and the other Mary to see the sepulchre. And behold, there was a great earthquake: for the angel of the Lord descended from heaven and came and rolled back the stone from the door, and sat upon it. His countenance was like lightning, and his raiment white as snow: And for fear of him the keepers

did shake and became as dead men. And the angel answered and said unto the women, Fear not ye: for I know that ye seek Jesus, which was crucified. He is not here: for He is risen, as He said. Come, see the place where the Lord lay. And go quickly, and tell His disciples that he is risen from the dead; and behold, He goeth before you into Galilee; there shall ye see Him: lo, I have told you. And they departed quickly from the sepulchre with fear and great joy; and did run to bring His disciples word. And as they went to tell His disciples, behold, Jesus met them, saying, All hail. And they came and held Him by the feet and worshipped Him. (Matthew 28:1–9)

By the apostles' testimony, we know Jesus Christ rose from the dead. Moreover, the apostle Paul tells us that Christ's resurrection is an indispensable component of our salvation.

For if the dead rise not, then is not Christ raised: And if Christ be not raised, your faith is vain; ye are yet in your sins. Then they also which are fallen asleep in Christ are perished. If in this life only we have

> hope in Christ, we are of all men most miserable. But now is Christ risen from the dead and become the firstfruits of them that slept. For since by man came death, by man also came the resurrection of the dead. For as in Adam all die, even so in Christ shall all be made alive. But every man in his own order: Christ the firstfruits; afterward, they that are Christ's at His coming. (1 Corinthians 15:16–23)

Therefore, the gospel (good news) of Jesus Christ is about receiving resurrection life and thus victory over death. Faith in Christ's resurrection assures us that we, too, will overcome death by the power of God, for our future resurrection is the complete fulfillment of salvation. As the apostle Paul explains,

> For this corruptible must put on incorruption, and this mortal must put on immortality. So, when this corruptible shall have put on incorruption, and this mortal shall have put on immortality, then shall be brought to pass the saying that is written, Death is swallowed up in victory. O death, where is thy sting? O grave, where is thy victory? The sting of

death is sin; and the strength of sin is the law. But thanks be to God, which giveth us the victory through our Lord Jesus Christ. (1 Corinthians 15:53–57)

But to believe in Christ's resurrection, we must believe in God's miraculous power. Like the resurrection, authentic regeneration is a miraculous work that only God can perform. Therefore, believing in the reality of miracles is crucial to believing in the soul and body's redemption. For this reason, Jesus performed countless miracles while on earth. These miracles give us faith in Christ's divine nature and prepare us to believe in His ability to raise the dead and remake the soul.

Thousands of eyewitnesses saw Jesus heal the sick. Many saw Jesus raising the dead. Multitudes watched Jesus miraculously feed thousands of people. By His miracles, Jesus Christ proved that He is the Messiah, who can raise the dead and give each sinner a new nature when they believe.

If your teeth are rotten and beyond repair, the dentist will suggest that you replace them with implants. Incorruptible screws are embedded into your jawbone so that new incorruptible teeth can be attached. And like thoroughly rotten teeth, people's natural hearts and souls are corrupt, as God explains:

> The heart is deceitful above all things,
> and desperately wicked: who can know
> it? (Jeremiah 17:9)

But the prophet Ezekiel gives us hope that God will miraculously implant a new nature into the hearts and souls of believers. For as the Lord said,

> And I will give them one heart, and I will
> put a new spirit within you; and I will
> take the stony heart out of their flesh and
> will give them a heart of flesh: That they
> may walk in My statutes, and keep Mine
> ordinances, and do them: and they shall
> be My people, and I will be their God.
> (Ezekiel 11:19-20)

In other words, being born again means God replaces your putrid heart with a new one that can respond to the Lord. And thus when the Spirit of God supernaturally implants resurrection life within your soul, you become born-again.

As a symbol of the new birth, Jesus Christ used the illustration of two wineskins.

> Nor do they put new wine into old
> wineskins, or else the wineskins break,
> the wine is spilled, and the wineskins
> are ruined. But they put new wine into

new wineskins, and both are preserved. (Matthew 9:17 NKJV)

Therefore, as with the new wineskin, God must give us a new incorruptible heart so we can contain the new wine of the Holy Spirit. And thus the Holy Spirit becomes our new heart, embedded in our new nature, to lead and guide us. Without this implantation of new resurrection life, one cannot legitimately claim to be a Christian. For as Jesus Christ said,

> Verily, verily, I say unto thee, Except a man be born again, he cannot see the kingdom of God. Nicodemus saith unto Him, How can a man be born when he is old? Can he enter the second time into his mother's womb, and be born? Jesus answered, Verily, verily, I say unto thee, except a man be born of water and of the Spirit, he cannot enter into the kingdom of God. That which is born of the flesh is flesh; and that which is born of the Spirit is spirit. (John 3:3–6)

However, every miracle Jesus performed on earth was temporary. All the people He healed eventually died. All the blind eyes Jesus opened became blind again in the grave. All the people Jesus miraculously fed became hungry again. And even Lazarus, whom Christ raised from the dead, died physically once again. But unlike His temporary miracles, the new birth in Jesus Christ never ends, and that makes the new birth the greatest miracle of all. For the miracle of regeneration assures us that we have eternal life, and one day we too will rise from the dead.

The new birth is an experience that all authentic believers have. To some, it comes softly and tenderly as they genuinely connect with the Spirit of the Lord and sense that their sins are washed away. To others, it comes in power as they experience the purging of sin and the Holy Spirit's impartation. Regardless of the experience, the new birth happens when you know God has supernaturally adopted you by washing away your sins. And thus the apostle Paul wrote,

> The Spirit himself beareth witness with our spirit, that we are the children of God. (Romans 8:16)

Likewise, this life-giving power of God is illustrated in the Gospel of Luke.

> And a woman having an issue of blood twelve years, which had spent all her living upon physicians, neither could be healed of any, came behind Him, and

touched the border of His garment: and immediately her issue of blood stopped. And Jesus said, Who touched Me? When all denied, Peter and they that were with Him said, Master, the multitude throng Thee and press Thee, and sayest Thou, Who touched Me? And Jesus said, Somebody hath touched Me: for I perceive that power is gone out of Me. And when the woman saw that she was not hid, she came trembling, and falling down before Him, she declared unto Him before all the people for what cause she had touched Him, and how she was healed immediately. And He said unto her, Daughter, be of good comfort: thy faith hath made thee whole; go in peace. (Luke 8:43–48)

At the glorious moment your faith touches the crucified and risen Savior, the resurrection power of God is transferred from Christ to you. And from that moment on, the Holy Spirit bears witness to your spirit that you are adopted, forgiven, born-again, and have everlasting resurrection life.

Chapter 14

Anchored to Sanctification

"I am not what I ought to be! Ah! how imperfect and deficient!—I am not what I wish to be! I 'abhor what is evil,' and I would 'cleave to what is good!'—I am not what I hope to be! Soon, I shall put off mortality: and with mortality all sin and imperfection! Yet, though I am not what I ought to be, nor what I wish to be, nor what I hope to be, I can truly say, I am not what I once was—a slave to sin and Satan; and I can heartily join with the Apostle, and acknowledge; By the grace of God, I am what I am!
John Newton
"The Christian Spectator" (1821)

If you love Christ, never be ashamed to let others see it and know it. Speak for Him. Witness for Him. Live for Him.
J. C. Ryle
"Do You Love Me"

As we have seen, genuine salvation is a miracle that comes only by God's power. And at the moment of salvation, God imparts a new spiritual mechanism or heart into the believer. This incorruptible nature is inhabited by the presence and power of the Holy Spirit. Henceforth, this tabernacle of grace cannot be lost or corrupted by any means.

But because this new nature starts small, it must be nurtured to grow in the grace and power of God. And therefore, just as a new wineskin can expand to contain the new wine, our new nature can develop and grow as we are filled with the Spirit of God. As the apostle Peter explains, we are "born again, not of corruptible seed, but of incorruptible, by the word of God, which liveth and abideth forever" (1 Peter 1:23). This new nature is likened to an incorruptible seed planted within our corrupt hearts. In effect, our old nature is invaded by a new container. And this container grows like a plant that transforms the rotten ground around it into a fruitful tree. But the growth of the new nature is not instantaneous. God must nurture and prune us over time to develop our spiritual maturity.

For this reason, Jesus Christ spoke to His followers about God's process of preparing His disciples for fruitful service. The word "disciple" means someone taught the discipline to follow the Holy Spirit's direction. Thus a disciple must learn to grow in faith and abide in Christ as God prunes away their selfish desires and makes them useful for God's evangelical purposes. For Jesus Christ said,

> I am the true vine, and my Father is the Husbandman. Every branch in Me that beareth not fruit He taketh away: and every branch that beareth fruit, He purgeth [prunes] it, that it may bring forth more fruit. Now ye are clean through the word which I have spoken unto you. Abide in Me, and I in you. As the branch cannot bear fruit of itself, except it abide in the vine; no more can ye, except ye abide in Me. I am the vine, ye are the branches: He that abideth in Me, and I in him, the same bringeth forth much fruit: for without Me ye can do nothing. If a man abides not in Me, he is cast forth as a branch, and is withered; and men gather them, and cast them into the fire, and they are burned. If ye abide in Me, and My words abide in you, ye shall ask what ye will, and it shall be done unto you. Herein is my Father glorified, that ye bear much fruit; so shall ye be My disciples. (John 15:1–8)

God's pruning work is unpleasant at times, for the old nature does not give up its desires easily. As F. B. Meyer commented,

> How often God takes away our consolations, that we may only love Him for Himself; and reveals our sinfulness, that we may better appreciate the completeness of His salvation![9]

As God prunes away our sinful proclivities and desires, we become productive witnesses of Christ's great salvation.

The apostle Paul identified two contrasting components operating within each born-again Christian, "the works of the flesh" and "the fruit of the Spirit."

> This I say then, walk in the Spirit, and ye shall not fulfil the lust of the flesh. For the flesh lusteth against the Spirit, and the Spirit against the flesh: and these are contrary the one to the other: so that ye cannot do the things that ye would. But if ye be led of the Spirit, ye are not under the law. Now the works of the flesh are manifest, which are these; Adultery,

[9] F. B. Meyer (1847–1929), May 12, 2022, https://www.ccel.org/m/meyer/homily/homily2.htm

139

> fornication, uncleanness, lasciviousness,
> idolatry, witchcraft, hatred, variance,
> emulations, wrath, strife, seditions,
> heresies, envyings, murders, drunkenness,
> revellings, and such like: of the which I
> tell you before, as I have also told you in
> time past, that they which do such things
> shall not inherit the Kingdom of God.
> (Galatians 5:16–21)

Notice how the actions of the old nature or flesh cannot enter the kingdom of God. Therefore, God is not interested in repairing the old nature which cannot get into heaven; instead, God wants to crucify and destroy the old nature by pruning it away. So for authentic born-again Christians, all the evil of their sinful souls will be destroyed when they die, but their new natures will enter the heavenly kingdom. Whatever transformation God's Spirit has invested into this new nature will enter heaven.

Therefore, God purposes to cut away the sinful branches of our old nature so the fulness of the Holy Spirit can manifest in our lives. And thus we are transformed when we focus on walking in the power of God's Spirit instead of exercising our flesh. As the apostle Paul wrote,

But the fruit of the Spirit is love,
joy, peace, long-suffering, kindness,
goodness, faithfulness, gentleness, self-
control. Against such, there is no law.
(Galatians 5:22–23)

This I say then, walk in the Spirit, and
ye shall not fulfil the lust of the flesh.
(Galatians 5:16)

In other words, when we live and focus on God's
will for our lives, sin loses power.

Hence, as we grow in the Spirit, God's goodness is
expressed through us. And the Spirit of God working
through us produces in us the nature of Jesus Christ.
Consequently, the nature of Jesus Christ in us will
create a desire to share our faith and serve others.

However, be reminded that God works through
the born-again Christian to produce charitable deeds
but our good works do not save us. Our good deeds
in Christ are the byproduct of a genuine Spirit-filled
life. The apostle Paul summarized the daily Christian
life in this way:

And those who are Christ's have crucified
the flesh with its passions and desires. If
we live in the Spirit, let us also walk in
the Spirit. (Galatians 5:24–25)

The apostle Paul also wrote that the daily Christian life is about dying to self and living for God.

> Likewise reckon ye also yourselves to be dead indeed unto sin, but alive unto God through Jesus Christ our Lord. (Romans 6:11)

Because of the cross, sin no longer can hinder us from walking in the Spirit of God. For at any moment, by the power of the Holy Spirit, we can change directions, receive forgiveness, and refocus our day on serving the Living God. Therefore, dying to self and living for God must be done daily. As Jesus said,

> If any man will come after me, let him deny himself, and take up his cross daily, and follow Me. (Luke 9:23)

Nevertheless, daily surrender to Jesus Christ can be a struggle. As an example, you may know that you cannot help a baby chick get out of its shell. Without the effort to break free from the shell, the chick will not be strong enough to survive. Some people, misguided by ignorant compassion, try to help the baby chick out by pulling the shell apart. But this inevitably leads to the death of the chick.

The struggle of the baby chick is similar to the daily battle for sanctification of every believer. God does not entirely remove us from our battle over sin, for He wants us to learn to grow amid the struggle. Therefore, it is normal for Christians to experience trials, difficulties, and setbacks as they battle their carnal natures. The battle teaches us to place our faith in Christ's power for success. The struggle with our flesh as our old natures resist God's will is like that of Jacob wrestling with God. But our new character, by ever-increasing faith, grows dependent on the Holy Spirit. And like any struggle, sometimes we stumble, for our greatest enemy as a Christian is our old nature.

Many Christians try to blame Satan when they sin, and in so doing, they focus on the Devil and not themselves. But ultimately, Satan is not to be blamed for our sin. Demons have the power to trick and tempt Christians to sin, but devils cannot force Christians to sin. And thus, when we sin, it is because we choose to sin. As the apostle James tells us,

> Let no man say when he is tempted, I am tempted of God: for God cannot be tempted with evil, neither tempteth he any man: But every man is tempted, when *he is drawn away of his own lust*, and enticed. Then when lust hath conceived, it bringeth forth sin: and sin, when it is finished, bringeth forth death. (James 1:13–15, emphasis added)

Part of us still wants to sin even after the new birth in Jesus Christ has saved us. But once again, the apostle Paul calls this part of us the "flesh," which is our old Adamic nature still active but diminished by regeneration. The fleshly eggshell still exists, and like the baby chick, we must spend the rest of our lives proactively pecking away at that sinful shell that entraps us in our rebellious lifestyles.

As we discovered in the last chapter, even though Jacob believed in God's promises, it took many years of struggle before Jacob walked God's way. Being saved and acting saved are two different things. When someone is born-again by the Spirit of God, we often expect them to perform in a perfectly suitable manner from the beginning. But this expectation is unrealistic, based on God's Word. Would you ask a newborn baby to run a marathon of twenty-six miles? Of course not. It takes years of natural growth and training to run a marathon. Therefore, we must balance our expectations of others with grace and not demand too much too soon. But we must also be people of truth who do not indulge people practicing willful immaturity and sin.

God wants people to actively grow in holiness and faith by learning to embrace their struggle over personal sin, for the Lord wants us to get past ourselves so that we can become blessings to others. We must be nurtured in God's Word and continually challenged to grow in the strength and power of the Holy Spirit.

And so the Christian life can be like walking up a down escalator: you must have the power to walk faster uphill than the speed of the stairs moving in the opposite direction, while our sinful nature acts as a down escalator still going in the wrong direction, continually leading us away from the good purposes of God. But Christians are always to move upward, and by the new birth, we have the potential to outpace the pull of the flesh. Therefore, our upward progression depends on our willingness to function in the direction and power of God. This dependence on God's power is called "resting in God" or "walking in the Spirit."

We resist our carnal selves' natural descent by prayer, Bible study, living a repentant lifestyle, and continuing in Christian fellowship, but upward progression in the Spirit must be our goal every day. For when we let down our guard, we descend morally by default.

Furthermore, we do not contend against ourselves alone as we travel upward on that down escalator. Worldly people who reject the new birth and God's will are moving down as we move up, and people moving away from God will resent you for moving in the opposite direction. They may hate you and try to intimidate you into changing course, and want you to join them in their downward trajectory of sin and rebellion against God.

Authentic Christians are contrary to the dominant

cultures of the world. For this reason, worldly people want Christianity to be repressed, degraded, and eventually eliminated. We should not be surprised when we suffer persecution for the sake of the Lord. When we fight our sinful condition and encourage others to do the same, we stand out as enemies of the dominant world system. But Jesus calls us to endure persecution as salt and light to the world.

> Blessed are they which are persecuted for righteousness' sake: for theirs is the kingdom of heaven. Blessed are ye, when men shall revile you, and persecute you, and shall say all manner of evil against you falsely, for my sake. Rejoice, and be exceeding glad: for great is your reward in heaven: for so persecuted they the prophets which were before you. Ye are the salt of the earth: but if the salt has lost its savour, wherewith shall it be salted? it is thenceforth good for nothing, but to be cast out, and to be trodden under foot of men. Ye are the light of the world. A city that is set on a hill cannot be hid. Neither do men light a candle, and put it under a bushel, but on a candlestick; and it giveth light unto all that are in the house. Let your light so shine before men, that they

may see your good works, and glorify
your Father which is in heaven. (Matthew
5:10–16)

This conflict with the flesh bears witness to others
that salvation comes to sinners like us only through
the grace of God.

Once saved, our purpose is to partake in the Great
Commission of Jesus Christ, for He came to save
souls and make disciples. Likewise, our mission is to
proclaim the new birth to all we encounter. So as we
head up the down escalator, we seek to turn people
around so they too can experience the new birth and
head upward in the power of God. For Jesus said,

All power is given unto Me in heaven
and in earth. Go ye therefore, and teach
all nations, baptizing them in the name
of the Father, and of the Son, and of the
Holy Ghost: Teaching them to observe
all things what soever I have commanded
you: and, lo, I am with you always,
even unto the end of the world. Amen.
(Matthew 28:18–20)

In other words, our mission in Christ is to tell the
unsaved to change course and receive the gospel of the

cross and the new birth, so they too can be redeemed by the blood of Jesus Christ.

For this reason, when a person has embraced the Great Commission, they need to be baptized, as commanded by the Lord, for Christian baptism is a dedication of oneself to live as a witness for Christ. A believer's baptism should happen the moment a person quits playing games with God and makes a lifelong commitment to live as Christ's evangelical ambassador. Authentic disciples fight the flesh, fight the lure of the world, and fight the Devil by continually sharing the Word of God so others can be saved. But unless we are dedicated to the salvation of others, our baptism is a meaningless gesture.

Which way are you heading? Are you going up the down escalator as a witness for Jesus Christ, or are you going downward with the flow of worldly people? If you are heading below, fall on your knees and get your heart right before God. Dedicate your life to Christ, receive the new birth, and embrace Christ's mission to save souls.

Chapter 15

Anchored to Heaven

Let not your heart be troubled: ye believe in
God, believe also in Me. In My Father's house
are many mansions: if it were not so, I would
have told you. I go to prepare a place for you.
And if I go and prepare a place for you, I will
come again, and receive you unto Myself;
that where I am, there ye may be also.
Jesus Christ (John 14:1–4)

Jesus Christ saves us to evangelize others. And thus, once we are genuinely redeemed, Jesus keeps us on earth for His ultimate evangelical purpose. Unfortunately, many professing Christians have little or no concern about the eternal destination of other people, for they falsely believe the primary mission of Christianity is to make this sinful world a better place. Instead of being primarily focused on evangelizing more people into heaven via the new birth, they have prioritized making the world a more prosperous or equitable place. And thus modern Christianity is about making people feel sad about the world's social, political, and economic state instead of feeling sad about individual lost souls. Therefore, they prioritize their time trying to save and befriend the wicked world instead of saving souls. But the apostle James tells us, "Whosoever therefore will be a friend of the world is the enemy of God" (James 4:4b).

However, if the Holy Spirit dwells within us, like God we will have divine compassion about the eternal fate of sinners, and we will be driven by God's Spirit to embrace the mission of Jesus Christ, who said, "the Son of man is come to seek and to save that which was lost" (Luke 19:10). Furthermore, we will understand that we too are commissioned to be witnesses of the gospel, for the gospel ultimately promises believers spiritual life in heaven with Jesus Christ, because He has prepared a heavenly place for us to dwell.

Unfortunately, the church's trend is to veer away from the central message of eternal life in Jesus Christ. But the scripture is clear that the gospel is primarily about being with Jesus after you die. For Jesus said,

> And if I go and prepare a place for you, I will come again and receive you to Myself; that where I am, there you may be also. (John 14:3)

But these days, heaven is an afterthought in many churches, and traditional evangelism is mocked. Many pastors promote straw man arguments against evangelism, saying, "Traditional evangelicals are heavenly minded but no earthly good," or "People who concentrate on getting people to heaven do not care about the conditions of people in the world." As a result, Christianity becomes a movement about social justice and economic reform instead of delivering people from eternal damnation.

But the facts do not support these straw man arguments. Historically, authentic evangelism, which prepares people for eternal life, has also raised the socioeconomic status, health, and education of every group it has encountered worldwide for nearly two thousand years because changes that enhance life are among the by-products of genuine salvation in Christ. Traditional evangelism has always made the world a better place. Born-again Christians become better citizens, workers, entrepreneurs, husbands, wives, children, and neighbors within their communities. Therefore, newborn Christians are wellsprings of blessing within their communities.

Furthermore, studies have proven that people who claim to be Christian but have no interest in traditional evangelism are no more generous than the general unredeemed population.[10] By contrast, conventional born-again evangelicals give most to charity. It seems that when churches no longer focus on eternal salvation, they create stingier people. And communities are hurt when fewer charitable evangelicals inhabit them.

The most significant thing we can do to impact the world is to redeem sinners, which changes lives in countless positive ways. It is therefore ironic that social justice Christians do little to help the poor and the oppressed and hence are similar to the Church of Ephesus. For Jesus said to them,

> Nevertheless, I have somewhat against thee because thou hast left thy first love. Remember therefore from whence thou art fallen, and repent, and do the first works; or else I will come unto thee quickly, and will remove thy candlestick out of this place, except thou repent. (Revelation 2:4–5)

Even though Jesus complimented the Church of Ephesus on its excellent doctrine, he rebuked them for losing their "first love," for they were dull in their love for God and thus dulled in their passion for saving others. Losing your love and passion for God affects

---

[10] "American Donor Trends," Barna Group, June 3, 2013, accessed May 12, 2022

your ability to witness the gospel enthusiastically, and apathy toward lost souls affects congregational health and purpose.

God pours out his power within a church for the express purpose of evangelism, and for this reason, the power and presence of the Lord are diminished when a church rejects traditional evangelism. But the Lord is with them who participate in the Great Commission. As Jesus said,

> Go ye therefore, and teach all nations, baptizing them in the name of the Father, and of the Son, and of the Holy Ghost: Teaching them to observe all things what soever I have commanded you: *and, lo, I am with you always, even unto the end of the world.* Amen. (Matthew 28:18–20, emphasis added)

The risen Lord Jesus warned the Ephesians that their candlestick, which represents the presence and power of the Holy Spirit, was in danger of being taken away because of their lack of love to fulfill the Great Commission. God does not empower churches when they neglect their primary calling to save souls. The Holy Spirit will depart from an organization when they no longer focus on getting people saved and bound for heaven when they die.

If you are born-again by the Spirit of God, then some things are certain about you. First, someone loved God enough, and you enough, to reach out to you with the message that Jesus saves sinners so you can dwell with Him in heaven. Second, the person who led you to the Lord was operating as an authentic evangelical disciple of Jesus Christ. Third, this disciple of Christ was willing to risk your wrath and rejection to share with you the good news that Jesus Christ died to take away your sins and that He rose from the dead. Fourth, this disciple was willing to tell you salvation comes only by the grace of God, through faith in Jesus Christ's atoning sacrifice. Fifth, this disciple was ready to deny their purposes and desires long enough to ensure that you were saved from hell, death, and the grave. And finally, this disciple was the product of a long line of faithful born-again witnesses that stretches back to Jesus Christ Himself, and thus hundreds of loyal disciples participated in your salvation. Therefore, the reason God gave you eternal life is so that you can pass that blessing on to others.

Do not be deceived. Even though our salvation is not based on good works, our reward in heaven is based on our efforts to save souls by the power of the Holy Spirit. For life to have eternal meaning, you must promote Christ, disseminate His truth, proclaim His salvation, and diligently work to deliver people from hell. Getting people to heaven is the primary goal of an authentic Christian. Evangelism is the divine mission of every legitimate Christian church.

As disciples of Christ, we must be willing to sacrifice our earthly life so that others will be saved too. But many are unwilling to sacrifice their comfort and riches for the souls of others, as Jesus Christ pointed out to the self-satisfied rich young ruler who wanted to know if he needed to do anything more to gain eternal life.

> Jesus said unto him, if thou wilt be perfect, go and sell that thou hast, and give to the poor, and thou shalt have treasure in heaven: and come and follow Me. But when the young man heard that saying, he went away sorrowful: for he had great possessions. (Matthew 19:21)

Jesus told the rich young ruler that purpose in life comes by following Christ, obeying His will, and helping others to do the same. But this rich man was unwilling to pay the price that Christian evangelism demands.

Once you become a born-again Christian, the Lord wants you to give up everything that hinders you from fulfilling His evangelical will, because you are called to be Christ's vessel of deliverance to others. As the epistle to the Hebrews says,

> Wherefore seeing we also are compassed
> about with so great a cloud of witnesses,
> let us lay aside every weight, and the
> sin which doth so easily beset us, and
> let us run with patience the race that
> is set before us, looking unto Jesus the
> author and finisher of our faith who for
> the joy that was set before Him endured
> the cross, despising the shame, and is
> set down at the right hand of the throne
> of God. For consider Him that endured
> such contradiction of sinners against
> Himself, lest ye be wearied and faint in
> your minds. (Hebrews 12:1–3)

Remember, hundreds of Christians have suffered persecution to pass on eternal life to you. Will you be the last link in the chain? Will you be like the rich young ruler who was so devoted to his things that he could not serve the Lord as a witness of eternal salvation? We must be willing to give up wealth, position, identity, racial pride, and even personal relationships to serve God's evangelistic mission. As Matthew records the words of Jesus about the cost of discipleship once we are born-again,

> Then answered Peter and said unto
> him, "Behold, we have forsaken all,

ANCHORED TO THE SAVIOR

and followed thee; what shall we have, therefore? And Jesus said unto them, Verily I say unto you, That ye which have followed Me, in the regeneration when the Son of man shall sit in the throne of His glory, ye also shall sit upon twelve thrones, judging the twelve tribes of Israel. *And everyone that hath forsaken houses, or brethren, or sisters, or father, or mother, or wife, or children, or lands, for my name's sake, shall receive a hundredfold, and shall inherit everlasting life.* (Matthew 19:27–29 emphasis added)

So are you feeling distant from God and Jesus Christ? Do you feel disconnected from the power of God? Then I remind you that the presence and the power of God are expressly given to make you a powerful witness for Him. Have you shared the good news of heavenly salvation lately? Are you actively telling people that Jesus Christ is the only way to receive eternal life? And when was the last time you proactively told someone about the atonement of the cross and the resurrection of the Lord? Does the eternal fate of others mean anything to you? If not, apathy toward soul-saving has separated you from His power.

Charles Spurgeon asked in his sermon "She Was Not Hid" (1888). "Have you no wish for others to be saved? Then he opined, "Then you are not saved yourself. Be sure of that." Can you legitimately claim to be God's child or filled with the Holy Spirit if you have little desire to see souls saved from hell? And if these realities do not disturb you, then it is likely you are bound for hell yourself, because the most significant evidence of genuine salvation is Spirit-inspired compassion for lost sinners.

I once preached a sermon where I asked the congregation to see the world through God's eyes. I said to them, "If you could look at a crowd of people walking to and fro, and you had the power to see with God's eyes whether they were bound for heaven or hell, how would you react? First, you would be shocked at how few are going to heaven. Because Jesus said in Matthew 7:13-20, 'Enter ye in at the strait gate: for wide is the gate, and broad is the way, that leadeth to destruction, and many there be which go in there.'

"Second, you would be shocked at how few professing Christians are willing to share the gospel or warn lost souls of their impending fate. Can you see it with your mind's eye? Most of your friends lost for all eternity. Most of your relatives lost for all eternity. And most of the people you work with lost for all eternity. Therefore, will you not lift a finger to help them? Will you speak to them about Jesus Christ crucified for their sins and raised from the dead? Will you warn them of the destruction to come, as your

Lord and Master did? Beloved, where is your passion and compassion for the unsaved?"

After the message, a visitor was upset with me, telling everyone who would listen to her that I was a disturbed man. And after some soul searching, I had to agree—people going to hell is a disturbing thing. But I am in good company, for God was so disturbed about man's sinful condition that He sent His only begotten Son to die on a cross. Jesus Christ was so concerned about hell that He left heaven to do something about it.

This disturbed Jesus took upon Himself the sins of the world, bearing in His body the righteous wrath of God. The apostles were likewise so concerned about sinners going to hell they willingly suffered persecution and martyrdom to save souls. God shares the reality of hell with us to disturb us into action against it, as only bothered Christians are motivated to proclaim eternal salvation in Jesus Christ.

As I come to the end of this book, I ask, Are you saved? Are you born-again? Have you been convicted of your sin? Have you grieved over your sin? Is Jesus Christ your Passover Lamb? Is the blood of the Lamb painted on the doorpost of your heart? Is Jesus your personal blood sacrifice? Has God personally removed your sins? Do you believe that Jesus Christ rose from the dead? Have you received the new birth? Have you been baptized in the power of the Holy Spirit? Do you fight with sin like someone going up a down escalator, or do you go with the flow? And finally, do you care about the eternal fate of others? If not, be honest with yourself. You have created an imaginary god to serve, for you are not born-again by the Spirit of God.

I challenge you to read the Gospels and the book of Acts with fresh eyes. See the early church's passion for winning souls to Christ. I call on you to humble yourself before God and cry out for true salvation—because when you die, you do not want God saying, "I never knew you: depart from Me" (Matthew 7:23). It is far better to hear Jesus Christ say,

> Well done, good and faithful servant; thou hast been faithful over a few things, I will make thee ruler over many things: enter thou into the joy of thy Lord. (Matthew 25:23)

About the Author

Patrick Edwin Harris has served the Lord Jesus
Christ as a pastor, evangelist, missionary, and prison
chaplain. He has led thousands to faith. His teaching
ministry is known for bringing clarity to biblical texts.

Printed in the United States
by Baker & Taylor Publisher Services